P9-ECN-060

RHEINGAU
Hochheim
Eltville
Rauenthal
Erbach
Kiedrich
Hattenheim
Hallgarten
Östrich
Winkel
Johannisberg
Geisenheim
Rüdesheim

RHEINHESSEN
Nackenheim
Nierstein
Oppenheim
Bingen

RHEINPFALZ
Wachenheim
Forst
Deidesheim
Ruppertsberg

MOSEL, SAAR, RUWER
Erden
Ürzig
Zeltinger
Graach
Wehlen
Bernkastel
Brauneberg
Piesport

FRANCONIA
Steinwein

SWISS
1. Neuchâtel
2. Vaud
3. Valais
4. Ticino
5. Zurich

ITALY
1. PIEDMONT
   Barolo
2. LOMBARDY
   Sassella
3. VENETIA
   Soave
4. EMILIA
   Lambrusco
5. TUSCANY
   Chianti
6. UMBRIA
   Orvieto
7. THE MARCHES
   Verdicchio
8. LATIUM
   Castelli Romani
9. CAMPANIA
   Capri
10. SARDINIA
    Vernaccia

MASSEE'S
Wine Handbook

MASSEE'S
Wine Handbook

REVISED EDITION

by *William Edman Massee*

DRAWINGS BY DOROTHY IVENS

Doubleday & Company, Inc.
GARDEN CITY, NEW YORK

ACKNOWLEDGMENTS

A book on wines elicits help from hundreds of people in the trade, members of official regulating bodies, growers, shippers, wine buyers, merchants—all of whom are called upon to verify facts, to correct errors of judgment, and to encourage the compiler of the book in general. For encouragement through the years, I am indebted to James Beard, author and epicure, as well as to Frank Schoonmaker, who is one of the world's best wine buyers and tasters; to Alexis Lichine, who first introduced me to wines; to Sam Aaron of Sherry-Lehmann, New York, who made many suggestions and provided me with countless labels; to Aaron Millman and Fred Burka, of Washington, who introduced me to the retailing aspects of the wine trade; and to many others in the importing and advertising and purveying branches of the trade. In Europe, the great help from the Director, Monsieur Pestel, and the Chief of Service, M. Devletian, and the staff of the *Institut National des Appellations d'Origine,* might well serve as an example of how cheerful and diligent are those who work for the cause of good wine. Most of all, of course, thanks must go to the honest vintners and growers who offer the essence of their skill and artistry to wine lovers everywhere, secure that there are many who will discern the wonders their wines contain.

For M.M.
who makes exciting
all things simple and good

Contents

CONTENTS

MASSEE'S
Wine Handbook

AUTHOR'S NOTE

In the lists of wines given throughout this book, the names of vineyards that are set in capital letters or boldface type are considered the best.

Vintage Lists

A NOTE ON VINTAGE CHARTS: Ratings of vintages for the great wine districts (see overleaf) are generally based on a scale of 20, great wines getting the highest numbers, which indicate what they will be like when the wines are mature. That's the catch, for ratings are made soon after the vintage, and many wines take a decade or more to mature. A great Bordeaux of 1970 may deserve a rating of 19 or 20 but won't reach that grand height until 1980. On the other hand, a great white Burgundy of the 1970 vintage will reach its peak about 1975. Consequently, the number on a vintage chart indicates only potential, and you need a line of development for each wine, so that it will be drunk when it is at its best. The chart overleaf gives some idea of which wines are ready to drink when.

The year 1970 is a good example of a large vintage of generally excellent quality. Fresh young wines like Beaujolais were ready to drink at the new year. Many of the Loire and Alsatian whites will be ready to drink in the fall of 1971. Lesser reds of Burgundy and the Rhone will begin to be drinkable during the spring of 1972. The great Burgundy whites will be ready the following spring. First growths of Burgundy and minor château bottlings of Bordeaux will appear on the markets toward the end of 1973 and will begin to be drinkable the following year; they will con-

11

RED WINE VINTAGES

VINTAGE	RATING	1970	'71	'72	'73	'74	'75
BORDEAUX							
53	16						
55	16						
57	14						
59	17						
61	20						
62	17						
64	17						
66	18						
67	15						
69	18						
BURGUNDY (Côte d'or)							
52	14						
53	14						
57	16						
59	18						
61	19						
62	18						
64	18						
66	18						
69	18						
RHONE							
55	16						
57	16						
61	18						
62	16						
65	14						
66	18						
67	18						
69	18						

18-20 = very great wines.
16-18 = great wines.
14-16 = good wines.

KEY:
...... First growth wines ready to drink. Great growths not ready.
——— Wines at their best. Great growths ready to drink.
- - - - - First growth wines passing their primes. Great growths beginning to decline.

WHITE WINE VINTAGES

VINTAGE	RATING	1970	'71	'72	'73	'74	'75
BORDEAUX							
61	18	······	······	······			
62	19		······	······			
66	16				······	······	
67	18						
69	16	······	······				
BURGUNDY							
66	18				······	······	
67	15				······	······	
69	19	······					
LOIRE & RHONE							
66	17				······	······	
67	18				······	······	
69	18	······					
RHINE & MOSELLE							
66	18						
69	18	······					
ALSACE							
66	17				······	······	
69	16	······					

tinue to be drinkable into 1980, when the great reds will begin coming to maturity. A great vintage like 1970 will have a rating of 19 or 20 and will provide a stream of wines for a generation. A few of the greatest bottles will last into the next century.

By Way of
Introducing Wines

Wines scarcely need an introduction these days, or so you might think if you go out to dinner in any bedside borough near any city. A bottle of Beaujolais or Pouilly-Fuissé usually makes an appearance, and something grander if you're lucky. Many a householder has a case or two tucked away, and when you walk into a store in Kansas City or Cleveland and don't see much of interest on the shelves, it's probably because the locals have bought them all up. Given a dock strike to slow up shipments or a bad year to put pressure on available stocks, and the shelves are swept clean in a week.

It's a sad state of affairs. Importers keep raising prices to keep abreast of prosperity; they bring in wines from a new Burgundy appellation called Hautes Côtes de Beaune or from a township unknown a decade ago, like Monthé-lie or Auxey-Duresses, and the wines are gone in a trice. That would be about two weeks. America has gone wine mad, and it's not all thirst.

Wine drinking is fashionable today. It's not at all a good thing. It was bad enough half a dozen years ago, when people bought good wines and drank them before they were ready; murdering babies, it's called in the import trade. It's worse, today. Wines that take ten years to get ready are marketed three years after the vintage. And Americans aren't known for patience. Practically nobody is prepared to store wines for seven years, waiting for them to mature. Suppose you are transferred to the other coast? Maybe the trip will hurt the wines. The consequence is that everybody is buying wines quickly ready to drink, forcing the prices up.

As if it weren't complicated enough, with all the different names. Now you have to shop for bargains, know the keeping qualities of various vintages, calculate drinking needs at least two years in advance, and have a storage space that will hold a dozen cases. It was all so simple when only a few were interested in wines.

Fortunately, the general quality of wine has gone up, what with controlled vinification temperatures and better vineyard and cellar controls. The volume of good wines has almost doubled in the past ten years, so that good wines in some volume now come from places like Portugal and California, where before were dribs and drabs or dreadfuls. It is true that some vintners have taken to sweetening low-priced wines to make them more palatable, a performance euphemistically called "softening," but they are drinkable today, where they were not ten years ago.

There's nothing to do about prices. My best advice would be to forget all about wines as long as you can, and if you get hooked on the delights of the grape, then find whatever is palatable at about two dollars a bottle, and be content. Don't become curious about estate-bottled Burgundies or château-bottled Bordeaux, ignore the joys of the Rhineland, pass up the California Cabernet Sauvignons and Chardonnays. Drink California Mountain Red, Chilean Riesling, Chianti in straw bottles, the occasional rosé. In no case, should you buy Champagne. The worst thing you can do is to learn to love wines costing ten dollars a bottle. Learn to like a few at three or four. Then stop.

It is true that few pleasures compare with the drinking of a fine wine, fully matured. But try to substitute other pleasures, like reading poetry, taking long walks, chasing women. It is quite true that there are scores of wines on the market for less than thirty dollars a case that are absolutely superb. The whites of Graves or the red Côtes du Rhône are examples. Some of the best California vintners have idiotically kept their prices down. Swiss wines are delicious, and almost unknown, as are Austrian wines. Many of the unknown château-bottlings of Bordeaux are still reasonable in price. Ignore them all.

Good wines only lead to great ones. And then you are lost. Look at the cost. You may start out by drinking a bottle or two a week, a Mâcon Rouge, say, or a little White Pinot from the Napa Valley. No harm in that. But then you will want to try a Volnay or a Chassagne-Montrachet, a St. Émilion or a Châteauneuf-du-Pape. Somebody touts you on an unknown château from Moulis, or a case of Muscadet at a ridiculous price. What's a case or two of wines a month? Then a friend has to move, and you take a few bottles off his hands, at a price. Or your local store closes out the last few cases of 1960 Château Talbot. Just where do you plan on keeping all that wine? A hall closet will do for a year. After that, you need a cellar. Aunts and in-laws used to be generous with cellar space. Now, they're all living in apartments and drinking wine themselves, which means they will steal your bottles. Friendly guardians of wine stocks are unregenerate thieves; the closer the relationship, the worse they are. Trust nobody. You will just have to build a cellar, or move above one.

Avoid others interested in wines as if they had social diseases. There is a camaraderie among wine drinkers that is fond beyond the telling. A wine lover has the strange delusion that his treasures are too good for ordinary mortals and is always on the lookout for a fellow amateur with whom to pull a cork or two. This leads to overeating and the consumption of bottle after bottle of good wines, a generosity you will wish to repay in kind. The pattern leads to overweight and great expense. To meet the cost you may cook up business deals together, the success of which will lead to more wine and more dinners. It is an endless round.

What's more, wine talk is boring. Vintages, and great discoveries, and subtleties of taste. Even women join the conversation today, wine being exciting, females becoming animated. That can lead anywhere. Wine drinking makes people sociable, and these days when privacy is so rare, we need to seek out solitude and inner contemplation. There's too much conviviality, altogether. You get so you don't even notice how dull wine talk is.

The purpose of this book, then, is to lead you to wines still reasonably priced. With it, you should be able to walk into any store and find the best buys readily. The finest wines are listed, but only as a warning. By all means, ignore them. Of course, if you want to taste something absolutely glorious . . .

18

The Various Kinds
of Wine

Wine, to begin with, is simply the fermented juice of freshly squeezed grapes.

But man has complicated matters in a marvelous fashion, vastly improving certain wines by additions to the fermented juice, so that four kinds of wine are made.

Add bubbles, and the result is a sparkling wine like Champagne, containing about 12 per cent alcohol.

Add herbs, and aromatic wines like Vermouth are made, which go up to 21 per cent in alcohol.

Add brandy, and the fortified wines like Sherry and Port are produced, which range from 14 per cent to 21 per cent alcohol.

Table wines have no such additions and range from 9 per cent to 14 per cent alcohol.

Sparkling wines, aromatic wines, and fortified wines are sold by brand names. The brands differ, depending on the stocks of wines held and the slight variations in the methods of blending and handling the wines. Table wines vary because of the soil, the grape, the climate, and the vine-tending and wine-making methods employed.

People are most curious about table wines, which are usually drunk at the table, with food. They are also known as light wines or still wines, because they are low in alcohol and have no bubbles. Red, white, or pink, they are known by place names and sometimes by the names of the grapes from which they are made. The best of them have the vineyard owner's name on the label, like the artist's signature on a canvas.

There is another kind of fermented drink that is not properly wine at all, made from the juice of fruits other than the grape. They are dubbed "fruit wines," and are made mostly from cherries, although elderberries, gooseberries, plums, and other small fruits are used. Hard cider, from apples, is a fruit wine, and so is perry, from pears. None of these fermented fruit juices can be transformed so marvelously into a liquid essence as can the juice of the grape, nor do they improve much with age, as grape wines do. The fruit wines are not usually drunk with food, as are the table wines.

But the table wines, simple and straightforward no matter how many subtleties they contain, are, above all, good to drink and easy to enjoy. What's confusing are their names and range.

The names are many and foreign, the range is worldwide. What's more, each region produces a variety of wines, from different grapes and soils, of varying quality. But the confusion is superficial and disappears when one understands the basic fact that table wines are classed as great, good, and ordinary.

Great table wines are so distinctive that they are sold under their vineyard names. Classed as vineyard wines, they often cost over three dollars a bottle.

These great wines generally live for five years and

longer. All the fine qualities of the grape are brought out. They come from vineyards that consistently produce exceptional wines, nearly all of which are in four European wine regions. In France, the Bordeaux and Burgundy regions produce great reds and whites. German vineyards, along the Rhine and its tributaries, and Hungary's Tokay region produce whites. Some long-lived wines are made along the French Rhone, in northern Italy, northern Spain, and elsewhere occasionally, but they vary in quality. Such regions are noted mainly for good, low-priced wines.

Long life, consistency, and all the other wine words attached to the great wines don't give much idea of what they're like. They're fabulous.

French troops salute the Burgundy vineyard of Clos de Vougeot to keep alive a tradition of respect that goes back a couple of centuries. The peace terms after the battle of Waterloo were eased for the French because their diplomats plied the treaty makers with Château Haut-Brion from Bordeaux, and a vineyard in the Moselle township of Bernkastel is called Doktor because a medieval bishop took a single sip of its wine and rose from his deathbed, not to heaven, but to drink the wine for a decade longer.

And the poets! Rabelais likened the Loire wines to taffeta because of their silky texture. Dumas said the white Burgundy of Montrachet should be drunk on the knees and bareheaded. The Apostle Paul was the one who said "a little wine for thy stomach's sake" was just the thing, according to the King James version, at least. So it has gone, down the centuries. But the only possible way to gain even the faintest inkling about such inspira-

21

tion is to pull a cork and lift a glass. No look is quite like the one that comes on a man's face after a drink of a great wine. It is as warming as the look of love, and as full of delight.

Good table wines, sold under the names of the districts or townships from which they come, are called regional wines. Usually drunk within two or three years of the vintage, they are the wines for regular drinking. The best of them cost around three dollars a bottle.

But these regional and vineyard wines account for less that 10 per cent of all wines. They are the aristocrats.

Most wine is simply pleasant to drink, what the French call *vin ordinaire*. The literal translation is misleading and derogatory, for the French mean by this a wine that is nothing to fuss about, a wine without subtlety, a wine that should be treated as casually as good bread or cheese, two other foods that also go through a fermenting process. Such a table wine, meant to be drunk without fuss or frills, is now often called a standard wine.

People who don't know much about wines should start with the standard reds and whites, to see what it's like to drink wine with food rather than water or tea, coffee or milk, beer or soda pop.

Wine drinking is a common pleasure, surrounded by nonsense. The welter of fake sophistication causes more people to turn away from wines than does the complexity of names. The attitudes are complicated, and it's all very discouraging to the man who wants a good glass of wine with his dinner.

Drinking wine is an adult pleasure. We Americans are lucky because so few of us drank wines while we were growing up, and our tastes aren't dulled by familiarity or lifelong prejudices. We can compare French, German, and Italian wines, for instance, with a certain impartiality, whereas a Frenchman is likely to insist any French wine is best, just as the German or Italian will uphold his native vintages.

The best way to become familiar with wines as a part of mealtime is to drink a glass now and then, perhaps two or three times a week. This might involve some modification of cocktail and highball drinking for most of us, but only to the extent of having one or two drinks before dinner, rather than more. The idea is not to add more alcohol to normal imbibing, but to replace some with wine. Many people like to begin by drinking wines on the weekends, but this is exercising an excess of caution.

This country produces a lot of good and pleasant standard wines, and the best of them are red. Many are sold under various French and Italian names, and cost perhaps a dollar a bottle, or less. In half-gallon and gallon jugs are such drinkable wines as "California Burgundy," "California Claret," "Vino di Tavola," and so forth. Slightly better wines are forthrightly called "Mountain Red," or "Napa Valley Red," and the best of all is usually "Zinfandel," named after the grape. They taste all right with meat and fowl.

Pleasant American standard white wines are called by such names as "Chablis," "Rhine Wine," or "Riesling," and come from New York, Ohio, and California. Those called "Mountain White" or those identified as coming from the Livermore, Sonoma, or Napa valleys in the San Francisco countryside are worth the few extra pennies they cost. These whites go well with fish and sea food, ham and pork, with fowl, with spaghetti or casserole dishes. Pink wines, usually called "Grenache Rosé," after the grape, go best with foods with which wines are served, and are chilled, like the whites.

After a gallon or so, having become used to drinking wines two or three times a week with all sorts of meals, you will find interesting others with more character. Lists and labels of regional and vineyard wines to try are in each section of the book. To try them, jot down two or three names that sound interesting, then go to the best shop in town and buy a couple of bottles, drinking the wines when the mood suits. Some people scribble their comments in the margins by the lists, making for themselves a personal guide out of this general one.

As to prices, those of French wines have jumped alarmingly over the past decade, reflecting increased demand by the prospering thirsty, Burgundy and Bordeaux having risen most. Prices quoted here are for wines as they come on the market in New York, which are generally representative. High cost of shipping or high local taxes, or high markups in cities where volume is comparatively small, tend to lift prices around the country to New York levels. State liquor stores may have bargains, but selection is usually small; large wine shops in competitive markets may buy in quantity and sell at reasonable prices a few of their most popular wines. Prices here are simply a relative guide, one wine or another being much higher or somewhat lower in any particular shop. As the supply of a great wine dwindles, its price climbs steeply, and a fine

Bordeaux or Burgundy from a fine vintage a decade ago may easily cost twenty dollars a bottle.

The good and great wines are generally in small supply and few of them fit into the economics of mass marketing. The minimum cost of shipping a wine and laying it down in a store is four dollars, and sometimes twice that. The importer and the wholesaler will each add 25 per cent or more to that laid-down cost, the retailer will add on top of that, 50 per cent to 100 per cent. The restaurateur may charge two or three times his cost. Large retailers often import wines directly, eliminating the markups of importer and wholesaler, but often paying higher prices for the wines abroad and paying premium prices for shipping and handling. Comparative shopping frequently uncovers bargains.

A rule of thumb may be helpful in reaching some sort of decision as to what one should pay for wines. One can figure that there are eight glasses in a bottle of wine, compared to sixteen drinks in a bottle of spirits, so an average price for a wine can be considered to be half that for spirits. For wines to drink from day to day, you might figure a cost a dollar below that average, with occasional splurges for wines that are a dollar higher. There is usually a 10 per cent discount on wines bought by the case; many retailers offer such discounts when you buy mixed cases of three or four different wines.

Reading Labels

"All I want is a good red wine that's cheap," people have been saying for 2000 years and more. As a result we're finally living in a golden age of wine, and good wines are made all over the world. But buying them is still a mystery. Would-be drinkers glare at all those labels on the shelves with indignation and dismay. "I'm willing to spend a couple of bucks for a wine to go with a stew or a steak. But not six dollars! Just name me a good red wine that's cheap."

A regional is what's wanted, a wine that bears on its label the name of the district where it's made. It will be what's called a good, sound wine, without sweetness and with the fruity taste of the grape. It will cost less than three dollars a bottle, in all likelihood, and will taste good with any meat or fowl, cooked any way. The ten best regional wines are probably those listed below.

SOME GOOD REGIONAL REDS

FRANCE		ITALY	SPAIN
Beaujolais	Bordeaux Supérieur	Chianti	Rioja
Chalonnais	Châteauneuf-du-Pape	Bardolino	
Mâconnais	Côtes du Rhone	Valpolicella	

California regionals are sold under names like Mountain Red, brand names, and grape names like Cabernet Sauvignon, Pinot Noir, Gamay Beaujolais, and Zinfandel.

AS PURVEYED TO THE HOLY SEE
Estate Bottled Red Rhone Table Wine

Chateauneuf-
ou-Pape

Appellation Chateauneuf-du-Pape Controllée

Saint Patrice

Antonin Establet et Fils S.A.
Négociants Eleveurs à Chateauneuf-du-Pape Vaucluse (France)
PRODUCE OF FRANCE

Typical regional label for Châteauneuf-du-Pape.

"I ask for one good wine, and suddenly there are ten. I can't even pronounce them."

But anybody can drink them with pleasure. The simplest way is to write down the names and take the list to the store. Most of them are in any good shop.

"Are they all the same?"

Not at all, but they're usually good and satisfying wines, on the same general level of quality.

"What about Bordeaux and Burgundy? At least I've heard of them."

27

Those two famous French regions produce great wines, most of which go to market bearing vineyard names. The area of southern Burgundy is an exception, most of the wines from there being labeled with district names, like Beaujolais.

"Can't you name me just one good red wine?"

Beaujolais, every time, if only one will do. A good wine is good to drink, goes the classic definition, with nothing unpleasant in the taste. Beaujolais is it. Fresh, fruity, sharp on the tongue, filling the mouth, it is the pet of France, the favorite young wine of all the world, at its best when less than two years old. Also good with cheese or chicken, veal or lamb.

"Spare me the details," says our sipper-to-be. "Just tell me what to look for on the label."

Name and date. The name, pronounced bo-zho-lay, shows where the wine comes from, and the date of the vintage shows when the wine was made. You need to know the date to be sure of getting a young Beaujolais, less than two years old.

"Suppose they haven't got any Beaujolais?"

Then buy a wine from another French district, such as Chalonnais, pronounced shal-awn-nay, which is right next door. Or a red from Italy, Spain, or California.

"Is that all there is to it?"

It's a starting point, and gets you going on drinking the good red wines.

"There's Beaujolais for a dollar ninety-nine, others for three dollars, and some for nearly four, all from the same year. What's the big difference?"

BIN 287

19..

Beaujolais

CHÂTEAU DE MONTMELAS

APPELLATION BEAUJOLAIS CONTROLÉE

MARCEL DESCHAMPS

NÉGOCIANT A MÂCON (S.-&-L.) FRANCE

A good shipper's Beaujolais, adorned with a fancy vineyard name, to add tone.

Wines vary from place to place. Some places are better than others. The name of the place on the label tells a lot about the wine and its worth, in a kind of shorthand. And if you can read one, you can read them all, if you know what to look for. Good labels to get to know are those on French regionals, particularly Beaujolais, because the wines are shipped all over the world.

Southern Burgundy has two other districts besides Beaujolais, the Côte Chalonnaise with several townships, and the Côte Mâconnaise, which ship wines as Mâcon Rouge. But Beaujolais ships an ocean.

The cheapest wines of the district are simply labeled "Beaujolais," and are brands from lesser vineyards. They are fair wines, better than those labeled merely "Burgundy," which are blends from the poorest vineyards in the whole region. Every wine bears the most specific label it can.

Slightly better vineyards than those whose wines are only entitled to be called "Beaujolais" produce wines that contain a half per cent more alcohol. They are entitled by law to be labeled "Beaujolais Supérieur." These two are the best cheap regionals one is apt to find in the average shop, which is something useful to know when looking at a shelf full of pretenders.

Still better wines have another name on the label, usually set in the same-sized type as "Beaujolais." This is the township, and identifies a wine from its better vineyards.

"You mean I have to learn the names of Beaujolais *townships?*"

Not necessarily. Just the presence of a town name is assurance of a superior wine.

"How specific does a label have to be?"

It has to tell you all you need to know. The district name, by itself, is enough for most regionals. Southern Burgundies are the exception, so good that each township produces distinctive wines. They ought to be called district wines or township wines, of course, but the world calls them regionals.

Like the best of Beaujolais, the best wines from the neighboring district of Chalon are also identified by town names. Other regionals don't go into such detail, although

30

From one of Burgundy's best shippers, but note the meaningless phrase, "dans mes caves," to suggest this good wine is better than it is.

they may bear words like "superior" or "great wine," in fancy lettering in the native language, to make the buyer believe the wine is better than it is.

Here, for instance, are the recognized township names of Beaujolais and Chalonnais. It is possible to find bottles from other townships in the district, but they won't be as good as those from the towns listed.

BEAUJOLAIS TOWNSHIPS		CHALONNAIS TOWNSHIPS
St. Amour	Juliénas	Mercurey
Chénas	Moulin-à-vent	Givry
Fleurie	Morgon	Rully
Chiroubles	Brouilly	Montagny

31

VIN DE BOURGOGNE – PRODUCE OF FRANCE

BEAUJOLAIS FLEURIE
"LES MORIERS"
19..

Mise en bouteilles au domaine – ESTATE BOTTLED
Mme MOUSSET, Propriétaire à ROMANÈCHE-THORINS (S&L)

APPELLATION D'ORIGINE CONTROLÉE

The vineyard name is unnecessary for this Beaujolais, but the owner thinks it worthy of estate-bottling.

To taste the ways Beaujolais can vary, which is a fundamental delight of any wine, it is helpful to know that Juliénas is often considered to be the outstanding Beaujolais, along with the slightly lighter St. Amour. Fleurie is the fruitiest of all, and the French favorite, fruitiness being considered one of the particular pleasures of Beaujolais. Chénas is also extremely fruity. Chiroubles and Moulin-à-vent are the fullest. Morgon lives the longest.

The quite similar Chalonnais is the lightest of the Burgundies, Mercurey being valued higher than the slightly lighter Givry and Rully wines.

No shop will have them all, but any good merchant will sell a mixed case of those he has, at the average case price. That's twelve bottles for the price of eleven, or thereabouts.

"What about vineyards?"

Vineyard names are important only on Bordeaux wines, those from Burgundy's Côte d'Or, and those from Germany's Rhineland and its satellites. These wines rate special attention, so much so that they are given special places on restaurant wine cards.

Proprietors proud of their wines may add vineyard names even to the wines of southern Burgundy and the Rhone. This may indicate superiority, because in any township there will be a vineyard slightly better than the others. But more often than not such names indicate an attempt to cash in on the cachet of the great vineyard wines. All that's really needed to buy a good regional is the district name. The French stretch a point in southern Burgundy, recognizing the superiority of the townships listed.

"Is that all there is to it?"

That's all. In France the right to use famous place names on labels is controlled by law, the *Appellations d'Origine*. Such controlled wines are the best from France, and are always identified on the label by the phrase *"Appellation Contrôlée."* This is a guarantee that the wine comes from the place it claims.

There's nothing difficult about reading a label. A glance can tell you if you are getting what you want. Considering the hundreds of lesser wines on the market, the glance is worth the effort, making it possible to buy a genuine, good wine, and not a fake masquerading as one of its betters.

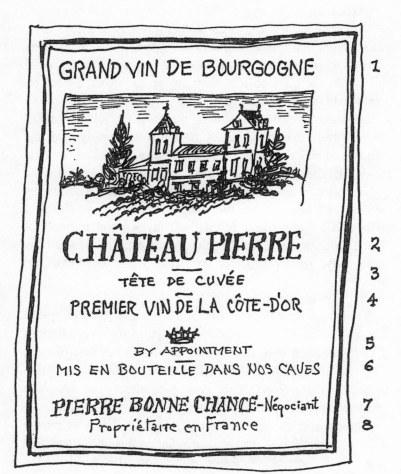

GRAND VIN DE BOURGOGNE   1

CHÂTEAU PIERRE   2
TÊTE DE CUVÉE   3
PREMIER VIN DE LA CÔTE-D'OR   4

BY APPOINTMENT   5
MIS EN BOUTEILLE DANS NOS CAVES   6

PIERRE BONNE CHANCE-Négociant   7
Propriétaire en France   8

FAKE LABEL

Nothing on this label tells you anything about this wine. The good and great wines of France are governed by vineyard control laws designed to reserve the famous names for the authentic wines. Those produced under this system always bear the phrase "Appellation Contrôlée" on the label. The phrase is omitted here, so the wine should be avoided. All the phrases are misleading:

1. The wine pretends to be a "Great Wine of Burgundy," but this is not a phrase recognized by the laws, unless accompanied by "Appellation Contrôlée."

2. Very few vineyards outside Bordeaux use the word "Château," and this word only has official meaning in Bordeaux. Wines actually produced at castles use the name, but here it is used to cash in on the cachet surrounding the word.

3. This phrase has no official recognition.

4. The Côte d'Or is a large area. The phrase "Premier Vin" has no official meaning.

5. This implies royal recognition, never of much significance.

6. This sounds like the legal estate-bottling phrase, but isn't. All wines are bottled in caves, or cellars.

7. This merely indicates that Pierre ships wine. Many do.

8. This says Pierre is an owner in France, but of what?

RED WINES
REGIONAL REDS

France has three famous red-wine regions; Bordeaux, Burgundy, and the valley of the Rhone. Bordeaux and Burgundy's Côte d'Or produce most of the French reds sold by vineyard names, while the area of Southern Burgundy sells most of its reds under district and township names.

The Rhone producers use district names too, and also blend the wines from lesser vineyards along the river, marketing them as *Côtes du Rhône,* Rhone slopes. These blends of wines vary from year to year and from shipper to shipper, but a better value under three dollars a bottle is hard to find. Here are names to look for on a label, from districts producing sound regionals. There are even some good regionals from the Loire.

FRENCH regional reds

BURGUNDY	BORDEAUX
Côte de Nuits-Villages	Graves
Côte de Beaune-Villages	St. Emilion or Pomerol
Beaujolais Supérieur	Haut Médoc or Médoc
Mâcon Rouge	Bordeaux Supérieur

RHONE	LOIRE
Côte Rôtie	Chinon
Hermitage	Bourgueil
Châteauneuf-du-Pape	St. Nicolas de Bourgueil
Côtes-du-Rhône	

36

Wines that are blends from various Rhone vineyards, entitled to this appellation, are excellent buys.

Côte Rôtie is in two parts, fruitier wines coming from the Côte Blonde than from the Côte Brune, whose wines are heavier. This is a blend of both, bottled by the owner in his own cellar—an estate-bottling.

37

"That's a lot of classifying."

It's a lot of wine, even though not much red wine comes in from the Loire because the French drink up most of the Chinons and Bourgueils. And scarcely 10,000 cases come out of Côte Rôtie. Consequently only the rest of the listed wines are names to remember. After you've drunk a few bottles, you'll wish there were dozens.

There are more, of course, because Bordeaux and Burgundy's Côte d'Or ship their regionals around the world, using minor district and town names on the labels. They are popular wines, and are consequently overpriced.

What's more, so much top wine goes into those sold with vineyard names, there's not much good wine left for the regionals. A wise buyer seeks out the vineyard wines, leaving regionals for everyday drinking. Even so, their general level of quality is high, like their prices. For the record, here's the list of districts and towns. To avoid repetition, descriptions of the vineyard wines of Bordeaux and Burgundy can be used for the regionals, minus superlatives, and will be found in that section.

BORDEAUX	*BURGUNDY'S CÔTE D'OR*
GRAVES	CÔTE DE NUITS
ST. ÉMILION	Fixin
POMEROL	Gevrey-Chambertin
HAUT MÉDOC	Morey-Saint-Denis
Margaux	Chambolle-Musigny
St. Julien	Vougeot
St. Estèphe	Vosne-Romanée
Pauillac	Nuits-Saint-Georges

BURGUNDY'S CÔTE D'OR
(cont'd)
CÔTE DE BEAUNE

Aloxe-Corton	Santenay
Pernand-Vergelesses	Volnay
Savigny-les-Beaune	Auxey-Duresses
Beaune	Monthélie
Pommard	Chassagne-Montrachet

The townships in the Bordeaux district of Haut Médoc market wines under their own names, which include Margaux, St. Julien, Pauillac, St. Estèphe, and Moulis. The best Bordeaux wines are marketed under the names of the various châteaux or vineyards.

"What about vintages?"

Like vineyard names, vintages are of importance primarily in France and Germany. Elsewhere the weather is generally fair enough to produce good wines. One year may be better than another, but this principally affects the size of the vintage.

The vintage year is needed on regional wine labels, though, in order to make sure the wine is the right age for drinking. Most regionals are ready for drinking as soon as they are bottled. Here's a list, followed by a detailed description of the regionals.

BEAUJOLAIS & CHALONNAIS
    Best when less than two years old.
CHINONS & BOURGUEILS
    Over two years, but less than five.
CHÂTEAUNEUF-DU-PAPE
    Over three years, not more than ten.
HERMITAGE & CÔTE RÔTIE
    Over four years, preferably older.
BORDEAUX & BURGUNDY'S CÔTE D'OR
    Over two, under ten.

The *Chinons* and *Bourgueils* are called typical *vins du pays,* country wines that were never shipped out of the Loire districts in the old days. They were thought to be too light to stand a trip, certainly not sturdy enough to stand an ocean voyage, which is supposed to add two years to the age of a wine because of the joggling and temperature changes. But new knowledge about fermentation and filtering, gained in the past decade, has changed all that. *St. Nicolas* is the fruitiest of the three, followed by Bourgueil and the light Chinon, which was one of Rabelais' favorite wines. All of them are at their best when less than three years old. They taste wonderful with light foods like cold chicken or veal, or slices from a leftover roast, or with cheese or a casserole. They may cost a little over two dollars a bottle.

Châteauneuf-du-Pape is the southernmost district of fine
Rhone wines, near Avignon. These big wines spend three
or four years in cask, and stay at their peak for five
or six years in bottle after that. They go particularly well
with stews and meat served with a sauce. *Hermitage* and
Côte Rôtie may rest in cask for seven or eight years, and
may need a couple of years more in bottle before they are
ready to drink, continuing to be good for a decade or
more. Hermitage is the biggest and fullest of French
wines, and one of the longest-lived, a perfect wine to
serve with hearty foods like a roast of beef, or venison, or
pheasant. Côte Rôtie is the fruitiest of all French wines,
at its best with fowl and game birds, with galantines and
terrines, and all kinds of rich meat dishes. All three may
cost five dollars a bottle, and while there is plenty of
Châteauneuf, to keep its price down, quantities of the
other two are small, to keep their prices up.

"Who wants to know about wines with pheasant? I
want to know about wines with steak."

All these wines taste fine with steak. But each has its
own distinction, special qualities that set it apart. Hermitage is marvelous with a sirloin, but it's even better with
rabbit stew; Côte Rôtie is marvelous with a filet mignon,
but it's even better with one of those cold meat loaves the
French call pâtés. Beef is good in different ways because
each way tastes distinctive. The same with these wines.

"I can't remember them all."

Ah, yes. The confusing names. To avoid them, most
people find a wine they like, then stick with it. One good
cheap wine, and that's enough. But a great deal of the
pleasure of wines lies in their variety, in the distinctive-

41

ness of each wine, region by region, district by district, town by town, vineyard by vineyard.

What's needed is some means of making the names stick in the mind, a foolproof device that will make it easy to remember any good wine. The best device is a corkscrew.

Nothing starts memory like a taste, a theme Proust so elaborately developed, and he began with a piece of spongecake. It's not easy to remember the taste of a specific wine, or even to identify a wine that one has tasted several times before. But there's no need to do so, wines not being made to be identified, but to be enjoyed.

The first taste of Beaujolais—or Bourgueil, or Côte Rôtie—is hard to forget. That moment will fix the name of the wine in your head forever.

Something in the taste of the wine will stand out—the fruitiness of the Beaujolais, the light freshness of the Bourgueil, the berry-like fullness of the Côte Rôtie—and with a little luck you are quite apt to remember that distinctiveness when you taste the wine again. You may not be able to name it, but through your head may flash a fleeting picture of a table, a companion, a dish, or the sound, or warmth, or light in a room. If someone then tells you the name of the wine, the very place and moment when you first tasted it will come surging back.

Here is one of wine's pleasures, wonders that come just because wines vary so endlessly. Hail the corkscrew and the delights of recall, caught again in the present instant.

"That's all very well, but you mean I have to spend a little effort. I just can't find one good cheap wine, and then that'll be it."

There's small joy in playing the same tune over and over again. What's more, the effort of buying a few bottles, followed by the task of drinking them, is generally considered exciting and pleasant.

At the same time there's no doubt that our attentive listener is disappointed. The first blow is finding out that a good wine costs perhaps three dollars and more. But cheaper wines are chancy. The second surprise is that wines seem to be so mysterious and perplexing, it's hard to believe that the number of good French regionals regularly shipped number scarcely a dozen different red wines. Pounce on odd lots you can find—a Cassis or Bandol from the Côte de Provence, for instance—because these are rarities. Even scarcer are country wines rarely shipped; some of the best of these are labeled VDQS, Vins Délimités de Qualité Supérieur, invariably pleasing to sample. Wines are simple, only the names are complex. To enjoy them, it is only necessary to give up some fixed ideas, and maybe an illusion or two.

Give up the idea that wines are somehow unknowable and only for the sophisticated; they are as simple and enjoyable as a fine day or a slice of good bread.

Give up the idea that wines are hard to buy; they are more clearly marked than any other product on the market.

Give up the idea that wines are hard to tell apart; they are as individual as members of a family.

Give up the idea that wines are hard to serve; all that has to be done is to pull the cork, pour into any glass at hand, and drink. Wine drinking is as simple as that.

The French regionals are fine wines to begin with.

ITALIAN regional reds

Wine buying is much harder for a returning tourist, used to drinking wines with every meal, than it is for the stay-at-home whose familiarity is limited to a few bottles on the shelves of the corner store. Wines are everywhere in Europe, galaxies of them, but a traveler is hard put to find any of them when he gets home.

The local wines, often good and delightful to drink in the excitement of travel and holiday, are rarely sent abroad because there's usually not enough to meet local demand. After a few days the traveler will recognize a couple of names that augment the local supply.

In a menu's purple ink will be listed "Bordeaux" and "Bourgogne." Costing perhaps a dollar a bottle, they are blends from minor vineyards, generally tasting biting and sharp.

"They taste sour," a tourist is apt to say.

Sour isn't the right word because a sour wine, *vin aigre* in French, is a wine that has gone bad. Vinegar is for salads, not for drinking. These puckery wines taste tart or astringent, which is not the same as tasting vinegary. They are also apt to taste watery, which is what winegrowers mean when they say a wine is too light, or lacking in body. The local wines may taste watery, too, and prickly and acid to the tongue, but they'll have a fruity taste and flowery smell that give them a fresher taste than the other two. Such a wine would cost a couple of dollars a bottle in the States, considering the cost of shipping, and would be worth it. But the wines simply called "Bordeaux" or "Burgundy" are not, even in France, because the best wines of these regions go to market under vineyard names.

When two of the most famous names in wine turn out to mean nothing at all on a label by themselves, a buyer is more than likely to throw up his hands and turn to Italy, where all wines are known by district or grape names. But in Italy it's the variety that's confusing.

There are more than fifty Italian reds that have made enough of a name for themselves to be called *vini tipici,* typical wines. The names are protected by law, and the implication is that they have a certain standard of quality or trueness to type. But the ways of wine making are so varied in Italy that any one name identifies a range of wines, light to full, good to poor. Price is the best criterion, if the merchant's buying knowledge is to be trusted. Most of these wines are cheap enough to make experimenting a pleasure. A really poor bottle is rare. Still, it can be confusing to find two different wines with the same name. Take Chianti, for instance.

Chianti is one of the glories of Florence, and young Chianti in the bulging, straw-covered *fiasco* is probably the most popular red wine on earth, the best being on a par with the best of Beaujolais.

But quite a different wine is made in the Chianti district, a wine that requires five or six years in cask and another year in bottle before it is ready to drink. Marketed in a regular wine bottle, it is an excellent wine, much like a good Rhone. Chianti is two wines, then, not one.

This doesn't bother the Italians at all. They seem to enjoy getting two wines from the same district. To avoid confusion, the big, full wines that need four or five years

ITALIAN
ROAST WINES

Barolo
Barbaresco
Gattinara
Carema
Valtellina
Sassella
Inferno
Grumello
Santa Maddalena
Chianti
Montepulciano
Nebbiolo
Barbera
Freisa

Italicized names are grape names, the Nebbiolo being used to make most of the fine wines of the Piedmont and northern Italy, and the Sangiovese being used to make Chianti. When old, say five years after vintage, some of the light table wines are also considered to be roast wines, among them being: Caldaro, Teroldego, Valpolicella, Valpantena, Sangiovese, Chianti, and

ITALIAN LIGHT TABLE WINES

Grignolino
Caldaro
Teroldego
Bardolino
Valpolicella
Valpantena
Lambrusco
Sangiovese
Chianti
Falerno
Vesuvio
Gragnano
Savuto
Ciro

Falerno. What the Italians seem to mean by this is that some of the ones classed as light table wines are ready to drink within two or three years of the vintage, but continue to develop for five years or so. The widely varying methods of vinification in Italy confuse the classifications. The neck stamp, above, signifies the wine meets government standards.

to mature are called "wines for roasts," *vini per arrosto*, on Italian menus, and are meant to be served with hearty roasts and stewed meats. Those that are ready perhaps two years after the vintage are called "table wines." The lighter table wines are usually served with all sorts of pasta—the spaghettis, macaronis, or noodles—and with all kinds of meat and fowl served with sauces.

Even this distinction is done away with in practice. If you want a big, full wine, you order an old "roast" wine; if you want a fresh and fruity wine, you order a young "table" wine. The Italians, particularly, believe that the right wine is whatever you like.

The best wines come from the north and from the vineyards around Naples. There are many cheap ones on the market, often good, but the top qualities cost between three and four dollars; a few are higher.

Barolo is by far the best roast wine of Italy, deep and full, needing at least three years in cask. Many people prefer the slightly lighter and faster-maturing Barbaresco, and many Italians insist that the more delicate Gattinara is the true aristocrat of the Piedmont, that vast region of northern Italy that produces the most distinguished of its wines. All are made from the Nebbiolo grape, which also produces the full and balanced wines of the Valtellina in the province of Lombardy, the best of which are Sassella, Grumello, and Inferno.

The outstanding light table wines of Italy are Valpolicella, Grignolino, and Bardolino from the north, Chianti, Lambrusco, and Sangiovese from central Italy, and Savuto and Ciro from the south. These are at their best when less than four or five years old.

As a group, they don't have the distinctiveness of the French regionals but are somehow friendly and cheering, just the wines for dishes that are hearty and full of taste.

A mixed case of Italian wines is a fine thing to have on hand when life is simple, appetites are large, and stews or pasta dishes are the foods you serve to a crowd. They are good wines for a buffet or a barbecue, for a sandwich lunch, for a pickup supper after a busy day. They are the perfect wines for easygoing American ways of entertaining, which may be why more Italian wines are sold here than any other. We buy too much Chianti and not enough of the others, though, and there are many to choose from.

SPANISH and LATIN AMERICAN
regional reds

There's no choice when it comes to Spanish red wines. There is only one important district, the Rioja, although some like to add the lesser wines of Valdepeñas. The Rioja, pronounced ree-O-hah, is a river valley planted with French grapes. Young wines from there are good. Old wines from the Rioja are often marvels; full, well-balanced, and subtle. The Spanish understand this very well, and keep almost all the old Riojas for themselves, making no effort at all to establish a world market.

The Spaniards set the pattern for South American wine making, using French grapes in the red-wine vineyards.

The only ones of these that come to this country are the Chilean reds, and these are often among the best buys you'll find in a wineshop. Like the Spanish reds, these usually cost at least two dollars a bottle, and go best with Mediterranean dishes full of taste.

CALIFORNIA regional reds

California was first settled by the Spanish, but other pioneers planted the French and Italian grapes as well, and these produce the best of the California red wines.

Most California wines borrow European names, so that there is much California "Burgundy" and California "Claret," the English name for Bordeaux, but these wines are rarely much good because they are heavily filtered, which helps to preserve a wine, keeping it from going bad, but also results in a wine that is flat to the taste, without any freshness. The wines that are so filtered are the standard wines, and are generally light and soft and insipid. They cost anywhere from under a dollar a bottle up. But bear in mind that about the minimum for a good one is around two dollars. They are like the ordinary table wines of Europe, but without their sharpness and intensity of taste. Some are sweetened.

The best California wines are marketed under the name of the grape variety, and are called "varietals," some costing under three dollars a bottle, a few twice that. Producers with national distribution are listed below. Try wines

50

of such small producers as Freemark Abbey, Hanzell, Heitz, Mayacamas, Mirassou, Robert Mondavi, Parducci, Sebastiani, Souverain, Stony Hill, and Weibel.

VARIETAL WINES

Cabernet Sauvignon	Pinot Noir	Zinfandel
Gamay Beaujolais	Petite Sirah	Barbera

VARIETAL PRODUCERS

Almadén	Concannon	Charles Krug
Beaulieu	Cresta Blanca	Louis Martini
Buena Vista	Inglenook	Paul Masson
Christian Brothers	Korbel	Wente Bros.

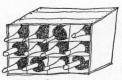

SAMPLE MIXED CASE REGIONAL REDS

Beaujolais	Barolo
Châteauneuf-du-Pape	Bardolino
Chinon	Capri
Hermitage	Napa Valley Zinfandel
St. Estèphe	Rioja
St. Julien	Valpolicella

VINTAGES: These districts produce consistently good wines, occasionally excelling in exceptional years, rarely failing except in years of excessive rain or drought. But vintages are important, because Beaujolais and Chinon are best when two years old or less, Hermitage needs five or six years to mature, while the rest reach their primes when three or four.

FOODS: All kinds of meat and fowl, stews, pastas and casseroles with meat or cheese, fish prepared with red wine, all cheeses.

SERVING: Should be opened an hour before serving. Best when slightly cool. Exceptions are Hermitage, St. Estèphe, or St. Julien, which should be opened a couple of hours before serving so that they can develop in contact with the air and warm to room temperature. These wines should be served casually and copiously, in generous glasses.

VINEYARD REDS

The world's finest red wines come from Bordeaux and Burgundy. The best of them are always sold by vineyard names.

In Bordeaux the word "Château" precedes the vineyard name on the label, to indicate that the wine was made at the vineyard by its owner. The system of labeling is sensibly called "château-bottling."

The same system is followed in Burgundy and elsewhere in Europe, where it is called "estate-bottling." The useful word "Château" is not used, but the names of the vineyards and their owners are, along with a gaggle of other words, to make things clear.

BURGUNDY

In Burgundy the name of the vineyard proprietor on the label is a guarantee of authenticity almost as important as the vineyard name. It signifies that the wine is estate-bottled. The grower's name usually appears in the lower right-hand corner with one of the following words, all of which signify he is the "owner" or "wine maker," and indicate that the wine was made by him:

> Viticulteur
> Vigneron
> Propriétaire-Récoltant

To make assurance doubly sure, a further phrase, like one of those below, is used to indicate that the wine was bottled at the estate:

Mise du Domaine
Mise en Bouteille par le Propriétaire
Mise à la Propriété

These are important phrases because not all wines from Burgundy vineyards are bottled at the property, by the owners. Many owners sell their wines to shippers, who have been known to blend the vineyard wines with others of lesser quality. The shippers try to cash in on the reputation of the estate-bottlers by using phrases that sound like the estate-bottling cachets.

A common fake phrase is *Mise en bouteille dans nos caves,* or a variant. This has no meaning, because all wines are bottled in *caves,* or cellars. A shipper may buy a vineyard so that he can claim to be a "propriétaire" on the labels of all his wines. But the word is only significant when the owner is a proprietor of the vineyard whose name appears on the label to identify the wine. These fakes are easy to identify, but they have to be looked for.

All the great Burgundies are estate-bottled, and take time to mature. The greater the wine, the longer it takes to mature. The great Burgundy reds usually spend less than two years in cask, but need three more years in the bottle to round out, and sometimes another five to reach their prime. Many are still drinkable after twenty years. Here is a list of the greatest Burgundies, the order in which they appear not necessarily being significant.

The great domain of Romanée-Conti always numbers the bottles of wine produced in each portion of vineyard it owns. Wines from the Great Growths frequently omit the township name as superfluous.

BURGUNDY *GRANDS CRUS*

Le Chambertin	Bonnes Mares
Chambertin-Clos de Bèze	Musigny
Latricières-Chambertin	Clos de Vougeot
Mazoyères or	Échézeaux or
Charmes-Chambertin	Grands Échézeaux
Mazis-Chambertin	Romanée-Conti
Griotte-Chambertin	Romanée-St. Vivant
Ruchottes-Chambertin	La Romanée
Chapelle-Chambertin	La Tâche
Clos de la Roche	Richebourg
Clos Saint Denis	Corton
Clos de Tart	

BURGUNDY VINEYARD REDS
SAMPLE MIXED CASE

Fixin	Aloxe-Corton
Gevrey-Chambertin	Pernand-Vergelesses
Morey-St. Denis	Beaune
Chambolle-Musigny	Pommard
Flagey-Échézeaux	Volnay
Nuits-St. Georges	Chassagne-Montrachet

VINTAGES: Vineyard wines from the above townships vary greatly in the time they take to mature. Those in the left column, from the Côte de Nuits, are rarely ready to drink until four years after the vintage, and most need another year or so to come into their prime. Those in the right column, from the Côte de Beaune, are usually ready to drink three years after the vintage.

FOODS: With all kinds of meat and fowl, but particularly with game, with roasts and grillades, and with stews. Perfect wines with cheese.

SERVING: These wines should be opened an hour or two before they are to be served, because they develop in the presence of air, as they warm to the temperature of the room. Four people can generally drink two bottles of these wines at a leisurely dinner. On such occasions, two different wines are often served, those from the Côte de Beaune being poured before those from the Côte de Nuits; the younger, or lesser, wine is served first.

56

In years when lesser vineyards make poor wines, these great vineyards are apt to make good ones. These wines are never bottled in years when they are poor. In fair years these vineyards may make exceptional wines, in good years these vineyards make outstanding wines, and in great years they make marvels.

Of the Burgundies, the *Chambertins* need five years to develop in good years, seven or eight to develop in great years, and are noted for their deep ruby color and their great fullness and depth of taste.

Clos de la Roche, Clos Saint Denis, and *Clos de Tart* are like the Chambertins but somewhat lighter, needing four or five years to develop in good years, perhaps six years to round out in great years.

Bonnes Mares and *Musigny* are noted for lightness and delicacy, often being ready to drink three years after the vintage but sometimes needing five or six years to develop in great years.

Clos de Vougeot and those called *Échézeaux* need five to seven years to mature, depending on whether the year is good or great, and are noted for their full, rich taste and great balance of qualities.

The *Romanées, La Tâche,* and *Richebourg* are noted for great balance, being called the queens of Burgundy when the Chambertins are called the kings, and need perhaps five years to develop in good years, ten years in great ones.

Corton is noted for its full, rich taste and fine balance, taking five years to develop in good years, a couple of years longer when the vintage is great.

All of them are good with all kinds of meat and fowl,

particularly with game birds and meats with full flavor, like lamb or venison. Because they are so expensive, one would drink a case of other wines to one bottle of these great ones, and they deserve to be reserved for times when a meal is an occasion.

Many of these wines are murdered, drunk up before they have reached maturity. They are sold as soon as they are bottled, and are quickly bought by eager drinkers who find it hard to wait until the wines are ready. On the other hand the English are famous for waiting too long, often twenty years or more, drinking the wines after they have lost life and vigor.

Impatient drinkers who can't wait ten years for a wine to become ready must turn to other vineyards, whose wines may be almost as magnificent but mature more quickly. These are called *Premiers Crus,* or First Growths.

In Burgundy all these great wines come from a narrow strip of vineyards, scarcely thirty miles long, called the Côte d'Or, the Golden Slope. All the best vineyards stretch in a line along this slope, just in the curve where the flatland meets the rise. Vineyards above and below this arc produce inferior wines, the vineyards out in the flat plains producing wines of the most ordinary quality.

The boundaries of each township run up and down the slope, from the ridge far out into the plain, so that a wine bearing simply the name of the township can often be less than ordinary, and usually is.

Toward the end of the last century, as world demand for the great Burgundies increased, the town fathers hit upon the shifty idea of adding to the name of the town the name of its most important vineyard. Gevrey became Gevrey-Chambertin, and so on along the slope, so that the magic names of great vineyards could be added to all wines from the township.

The misleading practice continues today, in spite of the fact that the great vineyards at the slope's bend are planted in the small-yielding Pinot Noir, while the plains vineyards are planted in the juicily abundant Gamay, which produces a really good wine in only one French district, the Beaujolais, where the sun is hot enough to bring out its best qualities.

Things are not quite so confused in Bordeaux, where all the top red-wine vineyards are planted in Cabernet and Merlot, grapes that give Bordeaux its character.

In both districts and in other leading districts of France, the name of the vineyard, the grapes that can be planted, and even the yield per acre are defined by law. These control laws even restrict the number of vines per acre and define the ways the vineyard must be tended and the wine made.

The control laws can't force a town to change its name to one that is less confusing. But the fraud committees that were set up under the laws are active in every district and see to it that the fair name of a fine vineyard is not used on an inferior wine. As an example, Le Chambertin is the name of the finest vineyard in the town of Gevrey, and the name is permitted to be used with the names of seven neighboring vineyards, whose wines are so close as to be almost identical; all of these wines are outstanding. But because the town has added the vineyard name to that of its own, wine marketed as "Gevrey-Chambertin" can be anything, and is usually an unexceptional wine.

A further complication is that the small Burgundy vineyards, many smaller than a football field, are divided among several owners, some of whom may own a portion scarcely the size of a tennis court. In a given year one owner may pick late and make great wine. Another, picking early, will make a poor vintage. This rarely happens, of course. But the wines of a single vineyard vary with the maker.

In most cases, however, the mere presence of a vineyard name on a bottle is enough to insure a superior wine.

In the following list only the vineyard names can identify a superior wine. The wines are arranged geographically, by town from north to south, those of one town being similar to each other and also like those from its neighbors. The vineyards of the Côte d'Or are divided in two, the wines from the Côte de Nuits, in the north, being fuller than those from the Côte de Beaune. The wines get progressively lighter as you move south.

The Great Growths, *Grands Crus,* are so famous that First Growths, *Premiers Crus,* are often passed up by the unknowing. Burgundy townships that have no Great Growths identify their best vineyards by calling them *Têtes de Cuvées,* chief vats, and these command higher prices than the others. In the following lists, the Great Growths are listed in capitals. Wines from vineyards not listed appear on the market now and then, and are generally of good quality.

CÔTE DE NUITS vineyard reds

FIXIN

La Perrière
Les Hervelets
Le Clos du Chapitre
Les Arvelets

These wines are on a par with the First Growth Chambertins, but are bargains because not so well known, rarely costing over five dollars. They need three or four years to mature in good years.

Mis en bouteilles au domaine — Product of France

FIXIN LES HERVELETS

1er Cuvée des vins fins de la Côte de Nuits
APPELLATION FIXIN CONTRÔLÉE

Pierre GELIN
Propriétaire à Fixin et Gevrey-Chambertin (Côte-d'Or)

This excellent label clearly names the vineyard in the township and identifies the owner as the wine maker in the "Mis en bouteilles" phrase. The vintage appears on a neck stamp and the cork.

GEVREY-CHAMBERTIN

Le Chambertin

Chambertin-Clos de Bèze

Latricières-Chambertin

Mazoyères or **Charmes-Chambertin**

Mazis-Chambertin

Griotte-Chambertin

Ruchottes-Chambertin

Chapelle-Chambertin

Clos St. Jacques

Les Varoilles

Cazetières

Combe aux Moines

Fouchère

Etournelles

A wine of Gevrey-Chambertin *must have* a vineyard name on the label to be outstanding. Clos St. Jacques is considered on a par with those allowed to place the word "Chambertin" with their own vineyard names. These are a bargain when under ten dollars a bottle. They take four years to develop when the vintage is good; another year or two when the vintage is great.

19..   MISE EN BOUTEILLE
AU DOMAINE

Cazetières
Appellation Contrôlée
Gevrey-Chambertin

DOMAINE
CLAIR-DAÜ
PROPRIÉTAIRE A MARSANNAY-LA-CÔTE (COTE-D'OR)

This simple label identifies an excellent wine of the township, an estate-bottling from a vineyard not rated as high as the first two listed above.

NOTE: There are many other vineyards in each township, and when the wines are bottled by the owner they are generally good buys.

MOREY-SAINT-DENIS

Clos de la Roche
Clos Saint Denis
Bonnes Mares
Clos de Tart
Clos des Lambrays
Meix Rentiers
Clos Bussière
Le Clos Sorbés
Les Ruchots
Les Millandes
Le Clos des Ormes
Monts-Luisants

The wines from Clos des Lambrays and Le Clos Sorbés are considered superior to the last four listed and command prices almost equal to the Great Growths. Not as well known as the Chambertins, these are often underpriced, perhaps seven or so dollars in a good year, when they need three years or so to develop, but a dollar more in great ones. The vineyard name (including others not listed) is assurance of a top wine.

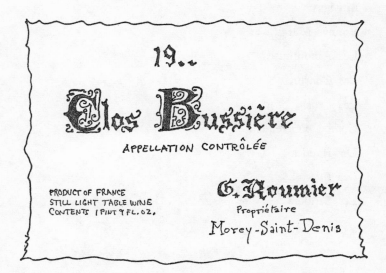

This vineyard, although not considered among the best of the township, nevertheless produces an excellent wine. There are vineyards in every wine township that are left off official lists, for such good reasons as that the wines are not like others in the township or because they vary widely from year to year. But many such vineyards are overlooked. Experimentation pays off surprisingly often, particularly when the vineyard is in a noted township and the wine is clearly labeled, as is this one.

CHAMBOLLE-MUSIGNY

Musigny

Bonnes Mares

Les Amoureuses

Les Charmes

Les Cras

Combe d'Orreau

Les Baudes

Les Fuées

Les Sentiers

Les Amoureuses and Les Charmes are superior to the last five wines listed.

More delicate than those to the north, these and those of other vineyards of Chambolle taste best with all meats and game, but particularly with meats served with a sauce, or with fowl. They take three or four years to mature in a fine year like '66 or '69, but four years or longer to develop in a great year like '61, when they cost twelve dollars and more.

66

The "Mise du domaine" phrase denotes this as a bottling of the estate by the vineyard owner but is shipped by a grower from the neighboring town of Morey-St. Denis, as indicated by the "Négociant-Éleveur" phrase and the address beneath. Although not listed above, it is one of several fine vineyards in this township, whose wines mature fairly quickly but begin to fade toward the end of the first decade after the vintage.

NOTE: There are many other vineyards in each township, and when the wines are bottled by the owner they are generally good buys.

VOUGEOT

Clos De Vougeot
Les Petits Vougeot
Les Cras

The large vineyard of Clos de Vougeot dominates this township, although some small vineyards are found outside its walled acres. The upper section of Clos de Vougeot produces the best wines.

FLAGEY-ÉCHÉZEAUX

Échézeaux
Grands-échézeaux

All the best vineyards of this township market their wines under the two names listed above, the appellations being classed as Great Growths.

VOSNE-ROMANÉE

Romanée-Conti   Aux Malconsorts
Romanée-St. Vivant   Les Beaux-Monts
La Romanée   Les Suchots
La Tâche   Les Gaudichots
Richebourg   Aux Brûlées
                               Les Chaumes
                               La Grande Rue

Overshadowed by their more famous neighbors, the Romanées, La Tâche, and Richebourg, the First Growths are often exceptional buys at seven dollars in a fine year like '66 or '69, when they need four years to develop. In a great year like '61, they are cheap at eight dollars, and need perhaps five years to round out.

Note that this wine is grown and bottled by the vineyard owners but that it is distributed by a shipper who has an exclusivity. The vintage appears on the neck label and the cork.

NOTE: There are many other vineyards in each township, and when the wines are bottled by the owner they are generally good buys.

NUITS-SAINT-GEORGES

Les Saint-Georges	Clos de Thorey
Les Vaucrains	Les Boudots
Les Cailles	Les Cras
Les Porrets	Les Richemones
Les Pruliers or Hauts-Pruliers	Les Didiers
Aux Murgers	Perrière

The largest township of the *Côte de Nuits*, Nuits-Saint-Georges produces much wine, and a vineyard name is assurance of a fine bottle. Full and rich, these wines need three or four years to develop, and are bargains when sold for less than six dollars. The first three wines listed are superior to the others.

PRÉMEAUX
(*marketed as* NUITS-SAINT-GEORGES)

Clos de la Maréchale	Clos des Grandes Vignes
Clos Arlots	Clos des Corvées
Clos des Argillières	Clos des Forêts

The many vineyards of Prémeaux add to the quantity of wine marketed as "Nuits-Saint-Georges." They are best buys when there is a vineyard name on the label, and cost less than six dollars a bottle in fine years like '66 or '69, or over six dollars in great years like '61. Perfect wines for all meats, particularly roasts, chops, and grillades.

MIS EN BOUTEILLE AU DOMAINE

APPELLATION CONTROLÉE

NUITS S.T GEORGES

Les Vaucrains

Domaine Henri Gouges à Nuits S.t Georges
(Côte-d'Or)   Bourgogne

This simple label identifies a fine estate-bottling.

NOTE: There are many other vineyards in each township, and when the wines are bottled by the owner they are generally good buys.

CÔTE DE BEAUNE vineyard reds

The vineyard name is enough to assure a fine wine. Listed here, under each township, are the largest vineyards and, therefore, the wines most generally available. But there are many other good vineyards in each township.

There are also some townships whose wines got lost in the shipper's vats, and whose vineyards were unknown. You might look for the following township names in the years to come: Ladoix-Serigny, Chorey-les-Beaune, St. Romain, Gamay, St. Aubin, Cheilly, Dezize, and Sampigny-les-Maranges. On the hills to the west are more vineyards, and these are marketed as Hautes Côtes de Beaune, not quite as highly considered as Côte de Beaune-Villages, which is a blend of wines from at least two towns of the district.

ALOXE-CORTON

Corton	Languettes
Les Bressandes	Les Pougets
Le Clos du Roi	Les Grèves
Les Renardes	Les Chaumes
Les Perrières	En Pauland
Les Maréchaudes	La Vigne-au-Saint

The appellation "Corton" can be applied to red wines from all the vineyards in the list, although the more specific vineyard name is frequently used. Big wines, needing three years to mature in a good year, four or five in a great

This estate-bottling could be called "Corton," but the owner chooses to identify the actual vineyard producing the wine.

one like 1969, these exceptional wines are noted for balance and fullness and are good with all meats, including game. They sell for seven dollars and up.

PERNAND-VERGELESSES

Îles des Vergelesses
Les Basses-Vergelesses
Creux de la Net
Les Fichots
En Caradeux

Not well known, and lighter and faster-maturing than the Cortons, these wines are ready in three years, usually, and are bargains when around four dollars a bottle.

73

SAVIGNY-LES-BEAUNE

Aux Vergelesses or Basses-Vergelesses
Les Lavières
Les Marconnets
Jarrons

A large township. Wines from its vineyards are excellent with all meats and fowl, including stews and meats served with sauces, and cost between three and four dollars a bottle, taking three years to mature. Vineyard names not *always* necessary.

Note that the Savigny is not shipped by the owner, but by a grower who bought the production, and yet the Beaune was bottled by the owners as indicated by "Mise du domaine" on a neck label.

BEAUNE

Les Grèves	Les Cents Vignes	Clos des Mouches
Les Fèves	Les Cras	Clos du Roi
Les Marconnets	Champimonts	Les Avaux
Les Bressandes	Les Theurons	Les Aigrots

Another large township full of vineyards. Many of the best wines are sold through the Hospices de Beaune auctions, where they command astronomical prices. When bought from producers, these soft, pleasing wines cost perhaps five dollars in a great year, slightly less in good years. Good with all meats and fowl.

Many Beaune vineyard parcels have been donated to the Hospices de Beaune, and these are sold under the name of the donor, as a cuvée, or vat. Some of the leading red wine cuvées are those of Nicolas Rollin, usually the highest in price of the Beaunes, although Brunet is rarely far behind, Dames de la Charité in Pommard, those of Charlotte Dumay and Dr. Peste in Aloxe-Corton, Général Muteau and Blondeau in Volnay. The famous whites are from Maursault, particularly the cuvées of Albert Grivault and de Bahèzre de Lanlay.

75

POMMARD

Les Rugiens, Bas or Hauts	Pézerolles
Les Épenots or Petits Épenots	Chaponières
Clos Blanc	Chanlins-Bas
Les Arvelets	Boucherottes
Les Charmots	Platière
Sausilles	Clos de la Commaraine

The fame of the name has raised the price of these soft, full wines, which can cost eight dollars a bottle in great years. Good with all kinds of meat and fowl, wild or domesticated. Vineyard names are necessary to get top wines. The first two vineyards are superior.

None of the red wines of the Côte de Beaune, with the exception of Cortons, are rated as Great Growths, but each town has its "chief vat," Tête de Cuvée. Both Rugiens and Épenots are so considered, and are the best wines of Pommard. This is the simplest possible label to identify an estate-bottling, the phrase beneath the owner's name stating that it was bottled by him at the vineyard.

VOLNAY

Clos des Ducs	Fremiets
En Caillerets or Caillerets Dessus	Le Clos des Chênes
En Champans	Les Angles, or
En Chevret	Pointes d'Angles

Another very famous township whose wines are at a premium because the name is so pleasing and so well known. Good wines with all meats and fowl. As with Pommard, the name of the vineyard on the label is particularly important. In a good year these wines can cost five dollars and more. The wines are soft and pleasing, perfect to serve to people who say they don't like wine because it's sour. Volnay is also good to serve to knowledgeable guests. The first three vineyards call for higher prices.

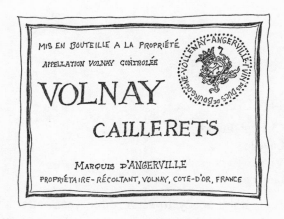

Note that on many labels the French article is often omitted before the vineyard name, although limiting adjectives like "haut," "petit," "bas," "dessus," and so forth are generally retained because they may indicate an entirely different vineyard.

MEURSAULT
(REDS *marketed as* VOLNAYS)

Les Santenots
Les Cras
Les Petures

A township famous for white wines, its reds are usually marketed as Volnays and are soft, full and pleasant wines, ready four years after the vintage. They generally cost five dollars a bottle in fine years.

MONTHÉLIE

Les Champs-Fulliot
Sur Lavelle
Les Vignes-Rondes
La Taupine

Pleasant, light, ready to serve three years after the vintage, these are good wines to serve for lunch, with meat casseroles and such. Should not cost much over four dollars a bottle in a good year, or even a great one. Vineyard names not *always* necessary.

AUXEY-DURESSES

Les Duresses or Bas des Duresses
Reugne
Les Grands Champs
Clos du Val

Almost as light as Monthélie, these are ready to drink three years after the vintage, and should cost around four dollars a bottle in a good year. A good wine to serve with cold slices off the roast, and with all sorts of meat sandwiches. Vineyard names not *always* necessary.

Note that vineyard names are not always necessary on wines from the minor Côte d'Or townships.

CHASSAGNE-MONTRACHET

Le Clos Saint-Jean	La Maltroie
Morgeot or Abbaye de Morgeot	Les Brussonnes
La Boudriotte	Les Champs-Gain

Another white-wine town, this one also boasts some distinguished reds, full and well balanced, bargains at five dollars a bottle in a fine year. The three last vineyards call for lower prices.

SANTENAY

Les Gravières
Clos de Tavannes
La Comme

Light wines, like those of Monthélie, come from Santenay, and should cost not much more than three dollars a bottle in a fine year. Vineyard names are not *always* necessary.

The Santenay is not estate-bottled, being a lesser wine, on a par with Monthélie.

BORDEAUX

There are eight First Great Growths of Bordeaux, equal to the *Grands Crus* of Burgundy. Many people believe that these are the greatest red wines on earth. They spend two or three years in cask, then may need five more years to develop. In great years they may not reach their peaks until ten years after the vintage, continuing to develop for another decade.

BORDEAUX *PREMIERS GRANDS CRUS*

Château Haut-Brion   Château Mouton-Rothschild
Château Margaux   Château Ausone
Château Latour   Château Cheval Blanc
Château Lafite   Château Pétrus

Of the Bordeaux reds, *Haut-Brion* is outstanding in mediocre years and truly incredible in years when the vintage is good or great. The wine is ready for drinking as soon as five years after the vintage. It is the great Bordeaux, invariably ready to drink before the others.

Margaux is the first of the great wines of the Médoc district to be ready, in a good year drinkable after five years, in a great year drinkable after seven or eight, coming into its prime at about ten years, and noted for its fullness.

Latour is the slowest-maturing of the great Bordeaux reds, invariably needing ten or a dozen years to mature, and distinguished by its great balance of fine qualities.

Lafite is distinguished by what the French call breed, finesse, and delicacy; takes seven or eight years to mature in a good year, ten or more in a great year.

Mouton is noted for fullness and balance, taking ten or twelve years to develop in a good year or in one when the wines mature quickly, but generally needing longer to round out in great years.

Ausone, Cheval Blanc, and *Pétrus* all produce exceptionally full wines, needing seven or eight years to develop in good years, a decade in great ones.

A typical label of a First Great Growth of Bordeaux.

Surrounding these vineyards are others that almost equal them, whose wines mature more quickly.

There is a century-old list of sixty-odd Médoc vineyards, a classification made in 1855 for a Paris fair, which is still more or less valid for use in identifying the top vineyards. In addition there is a list of more than a hundred vineyards rated as "Bourgeois Supérieur," plus a couple of hundred more that are called "Artisan," "Bourgeois," and "Paysan" growths, many of which go to market under vineyard names. These last three are often used in blends. There are some secondary districts from whose vineyards the skilled Bordeaux vintners can make good wines, and these, too, are used for the regionals.

HAUT MÉDOC

The Médoc is the greatest wine district on earth, producing more and better wines than any other, all the best of which come from the section nearest the city of Bordeaux called "Haut Médoc." Wines so labeled will be slightly better than ones called simply "Médoc," and because of this, other districts hopefully add "Haut" to their regional labels to make people think their wines are better than they are. The word is primarily geographical in the Médoc, and has no meaning as to quality elsewhere.

Here's a list of top Médoc vineyards, broken down by township. Those in capitals are the First Great Growths as listed in the 1855 classification, while the numbers following the vineyard names are the ratings according to that old listing. The numbers no longer have much meaning, many of the fourth and fifth growths having improved over the years, some of the second and third growths having declined. Any of these wines you can find will be superior.

Note that Chasse-Spleen is a Cru Exceptionnel in the list below and that it comes from Moulis, a town near Margaux. The numbered growths are generally superior, even though the rating is more than a century old. This is an excellent wine, in any case.

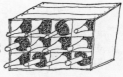

BORDEAUX VINEYARD REDS
SAMPLE MIXED CASE

Two château-bottlings, from different vineyards, from each of the following townships and districts:

Margaux	Pauillac	St. Émilion or Pomerol
St. Julien	St. Estèphe	Graves

VINTAGES: Some of these wines are ready three or four years after the vintage, but most of them are better when five years old, or older. Most of them are still in their prime ten years after the vintage. In poor years the First Great Growths often produce remarkable wines, which are sold at reasonable prices. The Great Growths are generally reasonable in price in good years, may be expensive in great vintages, like '64 or '66.

FOODS: With meat and fowl of all kinds, particularly those that are cooked simply or are served with light sauces.

SERVING: Open at least an hour before serving, to allow the wine to warm and develop in the presence of air. They are the wines to serve when the meal is light and the food is not too hearty or pungent. Particularly good with rich dishes that have a bland or delicate savor.

MARGAUX and its neighbors

Château Margaux

Brane-Cantenac II[1]

Cantenac-Brown III

Cantemerle V

Chasse-Spleen E[2]

Durfort-Vivens II

Ferrière III

Giscours III

Grand La Lagune III

D'Issan III

La Tour-de-Mons B[3]

Lascombes II

Malescot-Saint-Exupéry III

Palmer III

Prieuré-Lichine IV

Rausan-Ségla II

Rauzan-Gassies II

Château Angludet B

Bel-Air-Marquis-d'Aligre E

Boyd-Cantenac III

Dutruch-Lambert B

Fourcas-Dupré B

Fourcas-Hostein B

Gressier-Grand-Poujeaux B

Kirwan III

Lanessan B

Marquis-d'Alesme-Becker III

Marquis-de-Terme IV

Paveil B

Poujeaux-Theil E

Pouget IV

Du Tertre V

Villegeorge E

The wines from townships near that of Margaux share its qualities of bigness and fullness, and together these form the largest group of fine Médocs. Many of them cost between four and six dollars, the prices being lower in good years like the quick-maturing '67s and higher in great years like '69 and '61. The '62s and '59s are now ready to drink. Taste best with meats, and chicken or turkey.

[1] The Roman numerals indicate 1855 ratings.
[2] E stands for *Cru Exceptionnel.*
[3] B stands for *Cru Bourgeois Supérieur.*

SAINT-JULIEN

Château Beychevelle IV[1]
  Branaire-Ducru IV
  Ducru-Beaucaillou II
  Gruaud-Larose II
  Langoa-Barton III
  Léoville-Barton II
  Léoville-Las-Cases II
  Léoville-Poyferré II

Château Belgrave V
  Camensac V
  Lagrange III
  La Tour-Carnet IV
  Moulin-Riche E[2]
  St. Pierre-Bontemps IV
  St. Pierre-Sevaistre IV
  Talbot IV

Generally costing between four and six dollars, but rising to over eight dollars and more in fine years like '62, '64, '66, and '69, they are light and delicate, usually past their prime ten years after the vintage. Beychevelle has improved greatly in the past few decades, setting the character for the other wines to match; those in the first column are quite similar to one another. A mixed case of these wines is a good choice if beef, veal, and chicken are favorite meats. It's also a good choice because prices are low—that is, if you buy the lesser-known wines; those in the first column have become quite popular through the years, as has Château Talbot, now considered better than its 1855 rating.

[1] The Roman numerals indicate 1855 ratings.
[2] E stands for *Cru Exceptionnel*.

Although the 1855 classification rates this wine as Fourth Growth, in the past century its reputation has risen so that it is today considered on a par with the others.

PAUILLAC

Château Lafite
Château Latour
Château Mouton-
Rothschild II
Duhart-Milon
Lynch-Bages
Pichon-Longueville II[1]
Pichon-Longueville
(Comtesse de Lalande) II
Pontet-Canet V
Mouton-d'Armailhacq V

Château Batailley V
Clerc-Milon-Mondon V
Calvé-Croizet-Bages V
Grand-Puy-Ducasse V
Grand-Puy-Lacoste V
Haut-Bages-Libéral V
Haut-Batailley V
Lynch-Moussas V
Pédesclaux V
La Couronne E[2]

The township boasting more great Médoc vineyards than any other, Pauillac is rarely seen as a name on a bottle of regional wine. The wines are noted for balance and long life, and while the First Great Growths command twenty dollars a bottle and more in fine years like '62, '64, '66, and '69, the other wines can be bought for around five or so because they were underrated a century ago. Today they are among the best buys of Bordeaux. The First Great Growths may take two decades to mature, but the others are generally ready to drink ten years after the vintage. Good wines to serve with meat and fowl like chicken and turkey.

[1] The Roman numerals indicate 1855 ratings.
[2] E stands for *Cru Exceptionnel.*

90

SAINT-ESTÈPHE

Château Calon-
Ségur III[1]
    Cos-d'Estournel II
    Cos Labory V
    Phélan-Ségur B[2]

Château Mon-
Trose II
    Les Ormes-de-Pez B
    De Pez B
    Rochet IV

Costing often over five dollars a bottle, these are generally the fullest wines of the Médoc. The wines usually take ten years to mature and taste best with meat and fowl.

[1] The Roman numerals indicate 1855 ratings.
[2] B stands for *Cru Bourgeois Supérieur*.

SAINT-ÉMILION

St. Émilion vineyards were finally classified by the Apellations d'Origine committees in 1955, and the rather long list of First Great Growths and Great Growths is included here, although there are many others that produce good wines. St. Émilions are particularly the wines to serve with meat and fowl that have pronounced flavors. Like the Burgundies, they are good with game birds and meats. Ausone and Cheval Blanc may cost ten dollars or more in great years, but many others will cost half that.

PREMIERS GRANDS CRUS

Château Ausone
  Château Cheval-Blanc
  Beauséjour-Duffau
  Beauséjour-Fagouet
  Belair
  Canon

Château Figeac
Clos Fourtet
Château Gaffelière-
  Naudes
  Magdelaine
  Pavie
  Trottevielle

SAINT-ÉMILION *GRANDS CRUS*

Château L'Angélus
  L'Arrosée
  Balestard-la-Tonnelle
  Bellevue
  Bergat
  Cadet-Bon
  Cadet-Piola
  Canon-la-Gaffelière
  Cap-de-Mourlin
  Chapelle Madeleine
  Chauvin
  Corbin-Giraud
  Corbin-Michotte
  Coutet
  Croque-Michotte
  Curé-Bon-la-Madeleine
  Fonplégade
  Fonroque
  Franc-Mayne
  Grand-Barrail
  Grand-Corbin-Despagne
  Grand-Corbin-Pécresse
  Grand-Mayne
  Grand-Pontet
  Grandes-Murailles
  Guadet-St.-Julien
  Jean-Faure
  La Carte
  La Clotte
  La Clusière
  La Couspaude
  La Dominique
  Larcis-Ducasse

Château Lamarzelle
  Larmande
  Laroze
  Lasserre
  La Tour-Figeac
  La Tour-du-Pin-Figeac
    (Bélivier)
  La Tour-du-Pin-
    Figeac (Moueix)
  Le Chatelet
  Le Couvent
  Le Prieuré
  Mauvezin
  Moulin-du-Cadet
  Pavie-Decesse
  Pavie-Macquin
  Pavillon Cadet
  Petit-Faurie-de-Souchard
  Petit-Faurie-de-Soutard
  Ripeau
  Saint-Georges-Côte-Pavie
  Sansonnet
  Soutard
  Tertre-Daugay
  Trimoulet
  Trois-Moulins
  Troplong-Mondot
  Villemaurine
  Yon-Figeac
  Clos Des Jacobins
  Clos La Madeleine
  Clos Saint Martin

Chateau Fonroque

GRAND CRU

SAINT-EMILION

APPELLATION ST·EMILION CONTROLÉE

1953

◆ MISE ◆
DU CHATEAU

JEAN MOUEIX
Proprietaire
à SAINT-EMILION
(GIRONDE)

POMEROL

Château Pétrus	Château Certan
l'Évangile	Latour-Pomerol
Gazin	Nénin
La Conseillante	Petit-Village
Lafleur	Trotanoy
Lafleur-Pétrus	Vieux-Château-Certan

The wines of Pomerol have never been classified, so that many vineyards claim to be great vineyards. The ones listed are those that command the highest prices, Château Pétrus regularly commanding at least twenty dollars a bottle, while the others range anywhere from four dollars and up. Much fuller than the wines of the Médoc, often called the Burgundies of Bordeaux, Pomerols taste fine with all meats and fowl, including game birds.

Vieux Chateau Certan
Grand Cru
POMEROL
RÉCOLTE 19..
Appellation Pomerol contrôlée
Georges Thienpont,
propriétaire
MIS EN BOUTEILLE AU CHÂTEAU

GRAVES

Château Haut-Brion
Domaine de Chevalier
Château Haut-Bailly
  La Mission-Haut-Brion
  La Tour-Haut-Brion
  Latour-Martillac
  Pape-Clément

CHÂTEAU Bouscaut
  Carbonnieux
  Fieuzal
  Malartic-Lagravière
  Olivier
  Smith-Haut-Lafitte

These wines are good in fair years, excellent in good years, magnificent in great years, and wonderful whenever you can get them. They ripen early, are often ready when only four years old, and stay at their peak for a decade longer. Haut-Brion, like the other First Great Growths, often lives for twenty years and more. These are the perfect wines to serve with dishes that are served with a sauce, particularly chicken and veal, but they are also fine with simply grilled meats and fowl. Château Haut-Brion can cost twelve dollars and more, but the others generally cost between five and ten dollars, depending on the year.

LA GARDE

GRAND VIN
CHÂTEAU LA GARDE
19..

APPELLATION GRAVES CONTROLÉE

CLARET

MISE EN BOUTEILLES DU CHÂTEAU

Cru Exceptionnel

REGIONAL WHITES
SAMPLE MIXED CASE

Pouilly-Fuissé

Pouilly-Fumé

Vouvray

Muscadet

Alsatian Traminer

Hermitage Blanc

Soave

Orvieto

Neuchâtel

Steinwein

Chilean Riesling

New York Delaware

VINTAGES: These wines are best when about two years old and past their prime when five, generally, with the exception of Hermitage Blanc, which takes a year or so longer to mature, and can last for ten years and longer. Generally good wines, occasionally exceptional in outstanding years, and poor only in years of heavy rain, drought, or cold.

FOODS: With all kinds of fish and sea food, with fowl, with cheese dishes, with ham, pork, spicy meats, all kinds of delicatessen, and Oriental dishes.

SERVING: Before meals, and with light meals. Always best chilled, but if the wines are too cold, their tastes are masked. Bottles can be kept on the lower shelf of a refrigerator for days or can be cooled in an ice bucket in ten minutes.

100

WHITE WINES
REGIONAL WHITE WINES

Lots of people like to start on wines by drinking the whites, which are always served chilled because they taste better that way. They taste good with all kinds of fish and sea food and fowl, with veal and pork, with casseroles and cheese dishes. And perhaps they taste best of all with ham, sausages, pâtés, cold cuts, and all sorts of delicatessen. This may be because it's easy to take several swallows of a white wine, whereas the full, hearty red wines seem to taste better when they are sipped. White wines quench thirst better than reds, so they go well with spicy and salty foods, particularly Oriental dishes, and they are satisfying during the day without any food at all. A cool, beaded bottle on a hot summer afternoon, beneath the awning of a sidewalk café or on a shady terrace, is apt to be one of a tourist's fondest memories.

White wines are good to begin with because we are used to iced drinks, the familiar coolness counteracting the possibly alarming novelty of the white wine. Not so intense or full of taste as reds, they are less disturbing to people who are cautious about trying something new.

White wines are easier to become familiar with than reds because there aren't so many of them. For every white wine in the world there are ten reds, and once the tastes of a few of them have become familiar—say, those made from such grapes as Burgundy's Pinot Chardonnay, the Rhineland's Riesling or Sylvaner, or the Sauvignon Blanc of Bordeaux—you are familiar with most of the white wines on the market. Because they mature quickly—most white regionals are at their prime or past it five years after the vintage—they don't vary as widely or as subtly as the reds.

The number of white wines most people want to know about is still further reduced because many of them are sweet. Most sweet wines taste best when drunk with desserts. This is a limit on their desirability because people generally prefer to drink wines with other courses of a meal.

The dry whites are still a goodly number, however, and range widely from the hard, green, acid wines that are the pets of those who scorn any kind of sweet drink, through the flowery, fresh young wines that seem to hold spring in every sip, to the fruity, full, ripe wines that taste of summer. The luscious, lingering sappiness of a great sweet white wine is a delight to only a few, or on rare occasions, just as the acid sharpness of a parching dry white wine is not appealing to many. Most white wines fall between these two extremes, fortunately. These appeal to almost everybody. And the range makes easy the finding of favorites.

The greatest dry whites come from Burgundy, but many of the Swiss wines seem drier, being less full and more acid. The Rhine vineyards produce the most flowery whites, ranging from light and dry to full and sweet, while those from other French districts, from Italy, and from elsewhere around the Mediterranean and southern Europe are generally soft and often lacking in the acid that imparts a fresh and pleasing sharpness. Just about all of them are ready for drinking when two years old, although the best of them can continue to improve until the fifth year after the vintage. The life of most white wines, then, is from two to five years, in most cases the younger the better. The principal exceptions are the great dry Burgundies and the sweet wines of Bordeaux, the Rhineland vineyards, and Hungary's Tokay.

Dryness means absence of sweetness, although most people get the mistaken idea it means sourness. But alcohols have sweetish, flowery smells and tastes. The wine term "bouquet" refers to the collection of flowery aromas contained in a wine's various alcohols that are released when the alcohols evaporate. Wines also contain some oils and glycerine, which have sweet tastes. The driest of the Swiss and Burgundy whites consequently have a certain pleasing floweriness, which is offset by the wine's acidity. The variations in dryness are most easily noted in the white wines, because the range from dry to sweet is so much wider than in red wines.

The greatest white wines—the dry Chablis, Montrachets, Cortons, and Meursaults of Burgundy, the sweet Sauternes and Barsacs of Bordeaux, and the sweet and flowery Moselles, Rheingaus, and Rheinpfalzes of Germany—all go to market under vineyard names. They are always expensive. But the regionals marketed under district names are the wines for regular drinking, and the ones to get acquainted with first. Some of the wonders of the great wines are enjoyed from the first sips, but their subtleties and depths of taste are unrevealed unless one is familiar with the more apparent goodnesses of the fine white regionals.

103

FRENCH regional whites

France boasts some of the best regionals on earth. Full, dry whites come from districts in southern Burgundy and the Rhone Valley; lighter wines, dry or sweet, come from the Loire; flowery or spicy dry whites come from Alsace; and the mountain region of the Jura and Savoy sends to market a small galaxy of white, yellow, or straw-colored wines that range from dry to sweet. The most popular and best distributed are those from southern Burgundy and the Rhone.

BURGUNDY	RHONE
Pouilly-Fuissé	Château Grillet
Mâcon Blanc	Condrieu
Beaujolais Blanc	Hermitage Blanc
Rully	Châteauneuf-du-Pape Blanc

All of them are excellent first-course wines, perfect foils for a following red wine served with a roast, grillade, or stew. Vintages are more important as a guide to youngness than quality, generally. The wines usually cost between two and three dollars, a large crop meaning lower prices.

Best known of these is *Pouilly-Fuissé*, probably the most mispronounced wine name in the world. It goes pwee-yee fwee-say, more or less, which hasn't hurt its popularity and may help to make it easily remembered.

Like all the other white Burgundy regionals, Pouilly-Fuissé comes from southern Burgundy, is made from the Pinot Chardonnay grape, and is controlled by strict production laws. The laws limit yield per acre, so that extra vines cannot be crowded into a vineyard and so that excessive pressures will not be used in squeezing the grapes,

both of which practices increase quantity but reduce quality. But in good years grapes produce much juice, more than the lawful maximum, and unless the growers can persuade the local *Appellation Contrôlée* watchdog committees to increase the legal yield, the extra wine, *l'excès de production*, cannot be bottled as "Pouilly-Fuissé." The wine is marketed under the grape name, labeled "Pinot Chardonnay" or "Vin Blanc de Chardonnay," costs less than three dollars a bottle, compared to nearly four dollars for Pouilly, and is one of the best bargains in the world of wine.

Pouilly-Fuissé is the white peer of its neighbor, red Beaujolais. Pouilly is the classic wine to serve with what the French call *"charcuterie,"* products of the pork butcher that include all sorts of ham and pork and sausage combinations, similar to our delicatessen. It's a perfect wine to serve with cold cuts or a buffet; it's a fine wine for a picnic, the wine that comes to mind to suit the old expression "a bottle and a bird."

Mâcon Blanc and *Beaujolais Blanc* are like Pouilly-Fuissé, but without the fruity depth, so they cost less. Sometimes the township names appear on a bottle, to identify possibly superior wines. In the case of Pouilly-Fuissé, the town names of Pouilly-Vinzelles and Pouilly-Solutré are used, while Beaujolais uses the town names used on its reds. In the Côte Chalonnaise, *Rully* produces the best whites, although the towns producing reds also market some whites.

Château Grillet and *Condrieu* are two small vineyard areas near Côte Rôtie. The wines are dry and full, the peers of the neighboring red. Château Grillet is considered to be one of the great wines of France; a single large vineyard with a single owner, its wine is hard to find in the United States.

On down the Rhone, the large red-wine districts of *Hermitage* and *Châteauneuf-du-Pape* produce white wines almost as good as their reds. This is not unusual in red-wine districts, but the white wines rarely equal the reds. Hermitage, certainly, is an exception, for the whites are big and full, often taking four years to mature.

White Hermitage is a wine to serve when you want a white wine with wild fowl, or with rich or spicy ham or pork dishes. The white Châteauneuf is lighter and not so full, a good wine to serve with egg dishes that have a cream sauce—Eggs Benedict, for instance—and with curries, or other dishes that are apt to be served for lunch, with a salad.

Three other French regions provide France with a wonderful variety of white wines. The Loire offers at least half a dozen dry whites, plus the famous sweet Vouvray wines and those from the Anjou, Saumur, and Touraine. Alsace offers spicy Rhine wines made from German grapes, the spiciest of which is Gewürz-Traminer, while various districts in the Savoy produce a collection ranging from hard and dry to somewhat sweet and slightly sparkling, or *pétillant,* wines. Prices for many of them begin at just over two dollars, and rarely rise above four. They are perfect wines for all sorts of spicy meats, for freshwater fish, and for fat foods. Unlike the other two districts, Alsace uses grape names rather than district names to identify its wines.

LOIRE	ALSACE	JURA AND SAVOY
Muscadet	Sylvaner	Arbois
Pouilly-Fumé	Traminer	Crépy
Chavignol	Gewürz-Traminer	Seyssel
Sancerre	Riesling	Clairette de Die
Quincy	Edelzwicker	
Reuilly		
Partly sweet		*Sweet*
Vouvray		Château Chalon
Montlouis		L'Étoile
Saumur		
Anjou		

Muscadet, the driest wine of the Loire, from vineyards in Brittany near the river's mouth, is now perhaps the best of the inexpensive, good, dry white wines of France.

107

The best known of the Loire dry whites is *Pouilly-Fumé*, often confused with the similarly named Burgundy, but tasting different because it is made from the Sauvignon grape of Bordeaux. This light and fruity wine is also confused with wines from its lesser neighbor, *Pouilly-sur-Loire*,

which are made from the Chasselas grape. The nearby districts of *Chavignol, Sancerre, Quincy,* and *Reuilly* produce wines like Pouilly-Fumé that usually sell for under three dollars a bottle, less than their more famous neighbor.

Vouvray is the best known of the sweet, light wines of the Loire, so much so that the small neighboring district of *Montlouis* used to be permitted to ship its wines as "Vouvray." Both wines are always fresh and flowery, but range from almost dry to quite fruity and sweet in exceptional years. The wines of *Saumur* are similar, if not quite so light and fresh-tasting. The best sweet wine of the Loire comes from the township of *Coteaux du Layon* in the *Anjou*. It is marketed under its vineyard name, *Quart de Chaume*. All of these wines have a soft texture that caused Rabelais to call them *"vins de taffetas."*

Alsace is the only important French region that does not have vineyard-control laws, and the only one that markets its wine under grape names; Sylvaner, Traminer, Gewürz-Traminer, and Riesling. These wines have a flowery, springlike taste, the best being those made from the Riesling, although the French favorite is the spicy Gewürz-Traminer. Blends from various vineyards and of wines from various grapes are called "Zwicker" and "Edelzwicker," the latter being the better.

The mountains of the Jura and Savoy produce a variety of wines, perhaps the lightest, driest, and best being *Arbois,* followed by the similar *Crépy, Seyssel,* and *Clairette de Die.* An unusual yellow wine, left to mature in contact with the air to develop a tonic taste, is made at *Château Chalon.* Sweet straw wines, *vins de paille,* are made in *L'Étoile* by spreading the grapes on straw mats to allow them to dry. Both of these wines can live for decades, and are drunk as apéritifs or with desserts.

Vineyards near the Pyrenees produce a collection of sweet wines, rarely shipped, from such districts as Banyuls, Agly, Roussillon, Monbazillac, and Jurancon. They are called V.D.N. or V.D.L., *Vins Doux Naturels* and *Vins de Liqueur,* and like the wines made from the Muscat grapes and those from a cluster of minor districts, they are wines to taste when you come upon them.

Names, names, names. Well, start with the Burgundies, then down the Rhone, up the Loire, and up and down the hill vineyards of Alsace and the Jurals. After twenty bottles or so—spread over a few days, of course—you will be acquainted with a good cross section of the world's white regionals.

GERMAN regional whites

Moselblümchen	Steinwein
Liebfraumilch	Badischer
Frankenwein	Riesling

The only wines of distinction produced in Germany are white, from vineyards along the Rhine and its tributaries, the Mosel and the Main. Flowery and light, generally from 9 per cent to 11 per cent in alcohol, in great years wines with 12 per cent of alcohol may be produced by some great vineyards. Lovers of German wines like to drink them at any time of day, much the way one has a glass of beer. They are fine wines to serve with a light lunch, with ham, pork, sausages of all sorts, cold cuts, and fowl, fish or sea food.

Vineyard names are used to identify the top wines from the four greatest regions: the Rheinpfalz, which begins at the German border and runs north from Alsace; the Rheinhessen, which adjoins the Pfalz and extends north to Mainz and west to include the vineyards along the Nahe; the Rheingau, on the north bank of the Rhine, which crooks westward at Mainz; and the Mosel, which empties into the Rhine farther downstream at Coblenz. Only two of these regions ship blends of regional wines, the *Liebfraumilch* from Hessian vineyards, and the *Moselblümchen* from the Mosel.

German regionals are always dry and flowery, ready to drink the spring after the vintage and past their prime within three years. The vineyards are so far north that sugar dissolved in wine is added to the grape juice; along

111

with the natural sugar in the grape, this is converted into alcohol during fermentation. Without the added sugar, many of the lesser German vineyards could not produce wines with the desired minimum of 9 per cent alcohol, and in poor years this addition is necessary even in wines from many of the better vineyards. Because the sugar is converted to alcohol, it adds no sweetness to the wine; the technique is a common practice in Burgundy and elsewhere, particularly in poor years, and is carefully controlled by law. Many good wines, otherwise lost, are produced with this method. It is preferable, naturally, to make wines that depend only on the natural sugar in the grape. Such wine is called *"naturwein."* If the name of a vineyard and that of the owner appear on a German label, it is assurance that the wine is natural.

The German regionals generally sell for less than two dollars a bottle, although those bearing the names of townships may cost slightly more.

Moselblümchen, a blend of wines from lesser Mosel vineyards, is always light, dry, and somewhat flowery. *Liebfraumilch* is much fuller, and often has an earth taste, *Bodengeschmack,* that masks the floweriness. It is invariably made from the Sylvaner grape. It can vary from awful to pretty good, depending on the shipper and the price.

The full and dry *Frankenwein,* made from a variety of grapes, is perhaps the best cheap German wine on the market, although the wines vary from shipper to shipper. It is shipped in the stubby green *Bocksbeutel,* the name deriving from its similarity in shape to a goat's parts. Würzburg is the capital of the region, and its most famous vineyard slope, the Steinberg, has become a synonym for all Frankenwein. Wines from other towns along the Main are all loosely called *Steinwein* today, and the best of them may be bottled under vineyard names.

The wines of Baden are made from a variety of grapes, and while "Badischer" is familiar to the tourist as a good, fresh local wine, they won't be plentiful here for two or three years. They rank with Frankenwein, and may someday become the best German wine bargains available.

Riesling wines are made in every district, and because they are superior to wines made from the Sylvaner grape, the vintner is always careful to identify his regional wines made from the Rieslings.

113

SWISS regional whites

Neuchâtel	Lavaux
Fendant	La Côte
Johannisberg	Dézaley

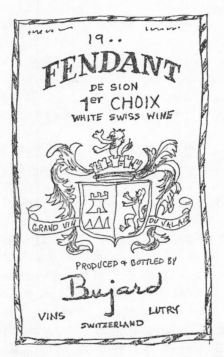

The light, dry white wines of Switzerland are superbly made and low in price, but they have never found much of a market here. Perhaps the fame of the French and German wines eclipses them, and yet their balance and lightness make them a good luncheon wine to go with fresh-water fish, cold cuts, cheese dishes, and so forth. They are fine for café drinking. Maybe our childish lack of cafés keeps consumption down, but with terraces and patios in half the nation's back yards, Swiss wines may come into their own.

Although every Swiss canton produces wines, only those from Neuchâtel, Vaud, and Valais are regularly exported. The wines are sold under canton and township names. Vineyard names are sometimes used, not so much for pretension's sake, but more to stress the fact that each wine has its own individuality. The prices of all of them are about the same, rarely rising above four dollars. The grape most widely used is the Chasselas, from the Loire Valley, although the Riesling, called here the Johannisberger, and other grapes are used, and the names sometimes get on labels. Fendant, incidentally, is the traditional wine for fondue.

SPANISH and other regional whites

SPANISH	MEDITERRANEAN	LATIN AMERICAN
Rioja	Retsina	Chile
Alella		

In the eighties French vintners went down to the valley of Rioja, in northern Spain, to see if they could grow the great French and German grapes, their own vineyards having been destroyed by the phylloxera, a burrowing louse brought into France on American wild-grape stocks. They introduced their vine-tending and wine-making methods, along with Cabernets, Pinots, and Rieslings, and began to make some good wines. They returned to France when the technique of grafting European vine stocks to

115

American roots was developed, now a standard practice in Europe. But they left behind their heritage.

Today all the best table wines of Spain come from the valley, including blends of several soft white wines, generally dry to moderately sweet. They are good wines to serve with paella, chicken with rice, and fish and sea food dishes. The wines should be young, not more than two or three years old, and should cost less than three dollars a bottle.

The Greeks and others around the Mediterranean have also adopted the wine-making methods developed to such perfection in France and Germany, and now they all produce pleasant, soft wines that range from dry to sweet. In Homer's time amphorae were lined with pitch to preserve the wine, and the Greeks continue the practice, adding resin to the wine to make *retsina*. It takes getting used to, by George, and travelers generally prefer the unresined wines. Like the other wines from Yugoslavia, Israel, Hungary, and Algeria, the Greek wines, resined or not, are so far only curiosities, worth trying if they are cheap enough.

That isn't true of Chilean white wines, made from European vines planted by the immigrants. The Chilean Rieslings are full and dry, if they are not more than three or four years old, and one of the best buys on the market. Bottled in the stubby *Bocksbeutel*, they often sell for two dollars or so.

ITALIAN regional whites

White wines are made all over Italy, and range from fairly dry to quite sweet. They are generally light in body but have a lot of taste, and are soft and pleasant with fish and sea food and antipasto. A length of salami, a wedge of Provolone, and a bottle of white wine make a good lunch.

Just about every district makes both dry and sweet white wines. The sweet ones are rarely exported, unless they are sparkling. The best of the dry whites are probably *Ischia,* from the island near Capri, *Soave,* from near Venice and sometimes better than Ischia, *Orvieto,* the peer of Chianti, and *Frascati,* the favorite white wine of Rome. There's a white Chianti, which can be good. These are pleasant wines, to drink without ceremony. Some of them, like Verdicchio, have an earth taste, which is not unpleasant if not too pronounced. Many of them have a seemingly sweet overtone of taste, due to lack of acidity in the wine, but this is not unpleasantly noticeable if the wine is well chilled. They should sell for less than three dollars a bottle.

ITALIAN
DRY WHITES

Capri
Colli Albani
Cortese
Est! Est!! Est!!!
Etna
Frascati
Gari
Ischia
Lachryma-Christi
Lugana
Orvieto
Sansevero
Soave
Terlano
Velletri
Verdiso
Verdicchio
Vermentino
Vernaccia

118

ITALIAN
SWEET WINES

Cinque Terre
Caluso
Greco
Malvasia
Moscato

Wines in italics are named after the grape.

AMERICAN regional whites

The soft and fairly light white wines from New York State are often called the Swiss wines of America, but they are quite different, having a distinctive and pleasant wild taste all their own. The best of them are made from hybrids or native American grapes like the Delaware or Catawba. The same holds true for the wines of Ohio and those from the Niagara Peninsula in Canada.

The California growers make good use of European varieties. Burgundy's Pinot Chardonnay makes the best white, followed by its cousin, Pinot Blanc, and Folle Blanche. Wines from the Sylvaner are called "Riesling" in California, and are pleasant and dry, but the best of the Rhine-like whites made in California come from the Johannisberg Riesling, which is what they call the true Riesling grape. Good dry wines from the Traminer are also made. The two white Bordeaux grapes, Sauvignon Blanc and Sémillon, produce pleasant, moderately dry wines in California. The Chenin Blanc produces a pleasant wine that's called White Pinot.

The best California whites are marketed under the name of the grape, and are called "varietals." The list includes the leading producers, whose varietals are generally available throughout the country, as well as the best grape varieties.

Wines are produced in several places in the East. Outside of Baltimore, a grape experimenter, Philip M. Wagner, produces a pleasant Boordy Vineyard White from hybrid grapes. There are other white-wine vineyards near San-

120

dusky, Ohio, and on nearby islands in Lake Erie, where the Catawba grape is grown, and there are vineyards in New Jersey, in Michigan, and on Canada's Niagara Peninsula, all producing wines of fair quality from hybrids and native grapes, the best of which are white. But the best eastern wines come from New York, and while grapes are grown along the Hudson and in Chautauqua County, the center of production is in the Finger Lakes region, centering around Hammondsport.

Native American grapes are domesticated versions of wild vines, and wines made from them possess a wild tang all their own. The climate is too harsh for European vines, but hybrid strains have been developed that will produce there a galaxy of new, distinctive wines in the coming decades. The old grapes, of which the best is the Delaware, followed by Catawba, still produce most of the New York varietal wines. The leading Finger Lakes producers are Widmer, Gold Seal, Taylor, and Great Western. They are perhaps best known for their production of excellent sparkling wines.

CALIFORNIA WHITE WINE VARIETALS

Pinot Chardonnay	Pinot Blanc	Semillon
Johannisberg Riesling	Chenin Blanc	Sylvaner
Sauvignon Blanc	Folle Blanche	Traminer

PRODUCERS OF CALIFORNIA VARIETALS

Almadén	Concannon	Louis M. Martini
Beaulieu	Cresta Blanca	Paul Masson
Buena Vista	Inglenook	Weibel
Christian Brothers	Charles Krug	Wente Brothers

121

VINEYARD WHITES

In some regions the white table wines are so good that they go to market under vineyard names. The very best of these will also have the name of the grower on the bottle, as a guarantee that the wine has not been blended or otherwise tampered with, a system called estate-bottling in every fine wine region in Europe except Bordeaux, where it is called château-bottling. This method of labeling is absolutely essential for identifying the great wines of France and Germany. It is possible that a great wine might be found on the market without the name of the vineyard and the grower, but this is unlikely. Even the secondary vineyard districts of the two countries, those districts where freaks of nature can produce great wines occasionally, follow the estate-bottling labeling system.

A great wine is classically defined as one that is characteristic of the place from which it comes, true to the type of wine made there, and long-lived. It must be long-lived so that the subtle secondary characteristics of the wine will develop after it has been bottled, something that can't happen if the wine declines quickly after being put in glass. Almost all the great white wines, those that can live three years or longer, come from the following districts and towns of France and Germany.

122

BURGUNDY	BORDEAUX	RHEINPFALZ
Chablis	Graves	Forst
Aloxe-Corton	Sauternes	Deidesheim
Meursault	Barsac	Wachenheim
Chassagne-Montrachet		Ruppertsberg
Puligny-Montrachet		

RHEINHESSEN	RHEINGAU	MOSEL
Nackenheim	Hochheim	Zeltingen
Nierstein	Rauenthal	Wehlen
Oppenheim	Erbach	Graach
Bingen	Hattenheim	Bernkastel
	Winkel	Piesport
	Johannisberg	
	Rüdesheim	

All these wines should be bought with vineyard names

BURGUNDY

Envy the man who is about to taste his first Chablis,
his first Corton, his first Montrachet. Even a man who has
never before drunk wines will feel bewilderment and delight, and though he won't be able to say why it tastes
so good, he'll be quite vocal about wondering where such
wines have been all his life. Still luckier is the man who
tastes such wines after having drunk a few other dry
whites and found them good, such regionals as Muscadet,
an Alsatian Traminer, a Swiss Neuchâtel, a Pouilly-Fuissé,
or a Hermitage. And if he tastes Chablis with oysters or
a brook trout, or Corton or Montrachet with a good pâté

123

or ham or fish served with a good sauce, his enthusiasm will be a pleasure just to watch. These three white Burgundies are the greatest dry white wines in the world, and drinking them is one of the fine pleasures of life.

Chablis comes from a separate small district north of the Côte d'Or, and the other great white Burgundies come from the southern half of the Golden Slope, the Côte de Beaune. Wines from both districts are marketed with the name of the vineyard on the label, although several fine wines are auctioned each year by the charity hospitals of Beaune, the *Hospices de Beaune,* and these are labeled under the names of those who donated the plots to the hospitals, and are sold as *"Cuvée* So-and-So." Many of them are overpriced, but it's in a good cause, for the hospitals take care of needy Burgundians.

The white-wine vineyards are small and are divided among several owners, so that an owner of small sections of several secondary vineyards may blend these wines and sell them under the name of the township, or under names like "Petit Chablis," "Chablis Villages," or "Beaune Villages." These are really regional wines, like those that are sold bearing only a township name, but because the control laws permit only the planting of the Pinot grape, they are generally of good quality. This is not true of many of the red wines bearing township names, because vines other than the Pinot can be planted in the lesser red-wine vineyards of the various townships. Estate-bottled wines, though—meaning those that bear the name of the grower on the bottle—are generally superior wines, whether white or red.

All the great white Burgundies are made from the

Chardonnay or Pinot Blanc, varieties of the same grape, and it is now believed that slight mutations in these vines from vineyard to vineyard may help account for differences in the wine. A Chablis is really not at all like a Corton or Montrachet, the slightest changes in soil or exposure bringing about differences in the wine.

The great growths, *Grands Crus,* of Burgundy are carefully protected by law, and the methods of vine tending and wine making are precisely defined. Wines from the *Grands Crus* always take two years to mature and often three, generally continue to develop until they are five years old, stay at their peaks until seven, and are past their prime ten years after the vintage. Many of them cost above five dollars a bottle, and a few of the greatest cost ten dollars and more.

The northern half of the Golden Slope, the Côte de Nuits, produces a small quantity of excellent white wines, particularly from a vineyard adjoining Clos Vougeot, the wine being marketed as "Clos Blanc de Vougeot," and from sections of the Musigny vineyards, but these are hard to find.

The great growths are easy to buy, and will always bear the name of the vineyard on the label. The very best will also bear the name of the vineyard owner, as a sign that the wine is estate-bottled.

BURGUNDY GREAT GROWTHS

CHABLIS

Vaudésir
Les Preuses
Les Clos
Grenouilles
Bougros
Valmur
Blanchots

CORTON

Le Corton
Corton-Charlemagne
Charlemagne

MONTRACHET

Le Montrachet
Chevalier-Montrachet
Bâtard-Montrachet

Criots-Bâtard-Montrachet
Bienvenue-Bâtard-Montrachet

VIN DE BOURGOGNE - PRODUCE OF FRANCE

ESTATE BOTTLED

BATARD MONTRACHET

RÉCOLTE 19..
Mise en Bouteilles au Domaine

Louis Poirier, Propriétaire, POMMARD (Côte d'Or)

APPELLATION D'ORIGINE CONTROLÉE

Note that the wine is not shipped by the proprietor of the vineyard, although it is made by him, and is shipped by a vineyard owner in a neighboring town.

126

The seven glorious vineyards of *Chablis* are on a single slope, less than ninety acres altogether, and the unique taste comes from the chalky soil, like that in the Champagne vineyards to the north. Everybody says Chablis tastes flinty, the way a struck flint smells, and while Burgundies are hunters' wines, and early similists had a musket in mind, we are apt to liken the taste of Chablis to the smell of a spent cigarette lighter, which is belittling to the wine's distinction. All such similes are confusing and inaccurate, especially when tastes are likened to the way various fruits smell, and when there's no real need to define the taste of a wine in words. It's all there, in the glass. I once told a wine expert Chablis tasted to me of dandelions and he said, no it didn't, Chablis tasted like Chablis and that was that, and he was right.

The *Corton* vineyards extend across two of the northernmost towns of the Côte de Beaune, Aloxe-Corton and Pernand-Vergelesses, so it was long ago decided to market the wine under the vineyard name and ignore the township name altogether. Only a part of Corton is planted in white grapes, so the name identifies both great white and red wines. The neighboring Charlemagne vineyard, once owned by the great conqueror, produces nothing but white wines, but some growers like to use the word "Corton" on their labels to insure proper identification. One of Burgundy's greatest shippers, Louis Latour, owns several parcels of the Corton vineyards that produce white wines, and he bottles them together, calling the wine "Corton-Grancey," which is always one of the top wines from the township.

Montrachet vineyards also extend across two townships,

Puligny and Chassagne, both of which add the vineyard names to their own. The vineyards bordering Le Montrachet produce such similar wines that those from the fifteen acres of Chevalier, which produce a scant 500 cases a year, from the fifty-five acres of Bâtard, and the four acres of Criots are all permitted to add "Montrachet" on the label.

The greatest dry white wine on earth is Le Montrachet, and while nearly a thousand cases of wine are made when the vintage is abundant, less than half reach the market, the rest being reserved by the dozen vineyard owners for their own pleasure. A bottle may cost twelve dollars, which is cheap.

These are wines to drink when only the superlatively wonderful will do. And because one must wait until four or five years after the vintage before the wines are ready, the only way to anticipate the marvels in store is to drink the First Growths, *Premiers Crus,* that begin to reach maturity two or three years after the vintage. Many of these are almost as good as the *Grands Crus,* and much cheaper because they are less well-known, more plentiful, and sooner ready for drinking, so that storage costs are lower. Corton is at the north end of the Beaune slope, Montrachet is at the south. In between are galaxies of glorious dry white wines, most of which must be drunk before they are five years old, almost all of which cost less than six dollars a bottle, and many of which cost less than four.

The districts of Chablis and the Côte de Beaune supply most of the First-Growth whites, although an occasional

fine white is made from Côte de Nuits vineyards, notably
in the townships of Chambolle-Musigny, Vougeot, and
Nuits-St.-Georges.

The First Growths of Aloxe-Corton, Beaune, Savigny-
les-Beaune and Pernand-Vergelesses are generally full and
golden, like Corton. Some of them do not bear vineyard
or township names and are sold as "Beaune Villages."
The First Growths of Meursault (which means "mouse
hop," because it is only that far from the red-wine vineyards of Volnay) are soft, with the color of straw, and
many Burgundians think they ought to be rated as *Grands
Crus*. Back in the hills are Monthélie and Santenay, whose
wines are light and soft, so unpretentious that many
growers don't bother to put vineyard names on their wines
at all. And in the towns of Puligny and Chassagne are
white-wine vineyards that produce vintages with the steely
quality and big body of the Montrachets; here, particularly,
the township name alone is assurance of a fine wine,
especially when the name of the grower appears on a
label. And a vineyard name is invariably enough to identify
a superior wine.

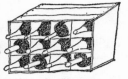

BURGUNDY VINEYARD WHITES
SAMPLE MIXED CASE

Two estate-bottlings, from different vineyards, from each of the following districts and townships:

Chablis

Pouilly-Fuissé

Aloxe-Corton

Beaune

Meursault

Chassagne-Montrachet

VINTAGES: These wines are ready to drink within two years of the vintage, usually, and past their prime at five, although the best may be good for a decade. The lesser wines of Monthélie and Blagny, for example, are unexceptional in years less than good, and even in great vintages they rarely last past their fifth year.

FOODS: Chablis is the classic wine with oysters, Pouilly-Fuissé is the traditional wine with delicatessen, but all of them are excellent with ham and pork cuts and dishes with all sorts of fish and sea food, hot or cold, and with spicy and pungent foods, including Chinese and Japanese dishes, curried and other Oriental dishes. They are frequently served with fowl of all sorts, and with cold dishes.

SERVING: These wines should be well cooled for at least an hour on the bottom shelf of the refrigerator, or in an ice bucket for twenty minutes. They are always served before red wines, because they are less full.

CHABLIS

Vaudesir	Montée de Tonnerre
Les Preuses	Fourchaume
Les Clos	Vaillon
Grenouilles	Beugnon
Bougros	Les Forêts
Valmur	Montmain
Blanchots	Côte de Léchet
	Vaulorent
	Mont de Mileu

Because there is so little of it, scarcely 500 acres, wines from the *Premiers Crus* of Chablis command prices almost as high as the *Grands Crus*. More than a score of vineyards are entitled to add the words *Premier Cru* to their labels, but only about half of these wines are exported.

131

Holdings are divided among many owners, and a vintner may choose to blend his small yields from his various First-Growth holdings, marketing them as "Chablis *Premier Cru.*" This is a not unusual practice in Burgundy, and such wines are worth looking for.

Chablis is particularly susceptible to frost and hail, so that little or no wine is made at times when other districts produce good bottles. The 1966 Burgundy vintage produced superior wines, and good '67s and '69s, although yields were not great. But no good wine was made in 1968.

The phrase *Premier Cru,* coupled with a vineyard name, is usually enough to insure getting an outstanding bottle.

CÔTE DE BEAUNE-VILLAGES
FIRST GROWTHS

Pernand-Vergelesses	Monthélie
Ladoix-Serigny	Auxey-Duresses
Savigny-les-Beaune	Blagny
Beaune	Saint-Aubin
	Santenay

These small townships of the Côte de Beaune occasionally market dry white wines labeled with names of their First-Growth vineyards, but usually only the town name is used to identify their best wines, while those from secondary vineyards are marketed as "Côte de Beaune-Villages." They are made from the Chardonnay and are

FONDÉE EN 1849

Savigny-les-Beaune

APPELLATION CONTRÔLÉE

Maison M. Doudet-Naudin
Négociant à Savigny-les-Beaune (Côte-d'Or)
Propriétaire de Vignobles
Mise du Domaine

The label indicates that this shipper augments the production from his own vineyards with those of others. Estate-bottling is not of great importance in the lesser towns.

generally light and quick to mature, ready to drink within a year. None of them will measure up to that southern Burgundy, Pouilly-Fuissé, which is often considered a great wine, and none of them should cost much over four dollars. In exceptional years, like 1966, they can surpass themselves, but they are rarely more than pleasant.

Some of the lesser vineyards of the Beaune slope are planted in the minor Aligoté grape, producing a sometimes pleasant white wine marketed as "Bourgogne Aligoté."

133

MEURSAULT

Perrières or Clos des Perrières
Les Genevrières
Les Charmes
Blagny

There are soft, dry wines with a full bouquet. Perhaps the reason they are not rated as *Grands Crus* is that they have a tendency to oxidize in the presence of air, acquiring a strawlike taste. The process is common to all white table wines, and is called maderization, because the wines take on the color of the wines of Madeira. The wine turns darkly golden, then brownish, giving the wine a brackish, stale taste. White table wines should never be more than golden in color, and are usually only lightly yellow or the color of slightly tarnished silver; a deeper color is often the sign of maderization, and such wines should be avoided.

A well-made Meursault from the top vineyards will not be apt to maderize during its first three or four years. All dry white table wines are apt to maderize before they are ten years old, which is why they are drunk when young. Maderization completely spoils the taste of a wine, and such a wine can always be returned, and should be.

NOTE: There are many other vineyards in each township, and when the wines are bottled by the owner they are generally good buys.

ESTATE   BOTTLED

Meursault-Blagny.

APPELLATION CONTROLÉE

Domaine Joseph Matrot

Propriétaire à Meursault
(Cote d'Or)

PULIGNY

Le Montrachet
Chevalier-Montrachet
Bâtard-Montrachet
Bienvenues-Bâtard-Montrachet
Le Cailleret
Les Combettes
Champ-Nanet
Pucelles
Les Chalumeaux

Because wines from the Montrachet vineyards are so rare, these First Growths are not only popular, but expensive. They are like the Montrachets, but are usually ready to drink at the end of the second year after the vintage. Part of the great Montrachet vineyards extend into the neighboring township of Chassagne.

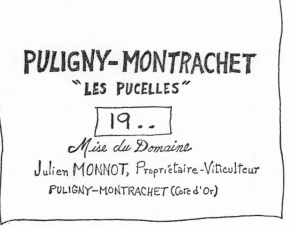

CHASSAGNE

Le Montrachet   Cailleret
Bâtard-Montrachet   Clos St. Jean
Criots-Bâtard-Montrachet La Boudriotte
Les Grandes Ruchottes   Morgeot

These wines also command top prices on the market, Ruchottes often surpassing Bâtard-Montrachet. They are more flowery than the Pulignys, and generally softer. Wine bottled as "Chassagne-Montrachet" is often an excellent buy because of the fine growers in the township who prefer to bottle their own wines rather than sell to shippers.

This is a good vineyard near Les Grandes Ruchottes.

BORDEAUX

While Burgundy produces only dry white wines, Bordeaux produces almost dry, soft wines from the Graves district and sweet, luscious white wines from the twin districts of Sauternes and Barsac. The best wines are always château-bottled, and are ready to drink two years after the vintage. The flowery Graves are usually past their prime after five years, but the sweet whites of Sauternes and Barsac last a decade and longer, although they are often past their prime after seven or eight years.

The top white wines of Graves were officially classified in 1953.

Eight vineyards are now rated as *Crus Classés,* and these Great Growths generally produce flowery wines that are particularly good with fish, sea food, and ham. These top wines invariably cost four dollars a bottle, but there are many other château-bottled whites available for around three dollars, many of which are excellent. These are among the best buys in the world of wine. One of the driest Graves whites comes from Château Haut-Brion.

GRAVES vineyard whites

Château Haut-Brion
Bouscaut
Carbonnieux
Chevalier
Olivier
Malartic-Lagravière
Laville-Haut-Brion
Couhins
La Tour-Martillac

138

OLIVIER

CHATEAU OLIVIER

1ᵉʳ CRU DÉPOSÉ GRAVES
France
MISE EN BOUTEILLES DU CHATEAU
PRINTED IN FRANCE

VIN DE BORDEAUX
CONTENTS 1 PT. 8 FL OZ ALCOHOLICSTRG AMIBICL
PRODUCED BOTTLED & SHIPPED BY
LOUIS ESCHENAUER
BORDEAUX (FRANCE)

139

SAUTERNES vineyard whites

A great amount of regional wine is produced in Sauternes and Barsac, but more than a score of the top vineyards were rated in 1855, and dozens more are château-bottled, so there is little point in buying the lesser wines that go to market under the district names. The name "Haut Sauternes" is often seen on a bottle and is supposed to indicate a superior wine, or a sweeter one, but does not. The phrase is a beguiling shippers' way to imply a superiority that does not exist.

All Sauternes and Barsac should be sweet, the sweeter the greater. The outstanding wine is that of Château d'Yquem, although La Tour-Blanche, Climens, and Filhot are close behind. The grapes are not picked until a mold, called the *pourriture noble,* or noble rot, forms on the skin of the grape. The vineyards are picked several times, the vintage sometimes continuing into December. These rich white wines are considered by many to be the greatest sweet wines in the world, only occasionally being equaled by wines made from similarly late-picked grapes from the Rhineland vineyards and Hungary's Tokay district. These wines are often served with lobster, crab, and fish that have a sweet savor, but they are perhaps best appreciated with rich pastries, and desserts like chocolate mousse. Best recent vintages are '66, the less-sweet '67s, and the luscious '61s and '62s.

SAUTERNES AND BARSAC

Château D'Yquem	Coutet
Château La Tour Blanche	Climens
Lafaurie-Peyraguey	Guiraud
Haut-Peyraguey	Rieussec
Rayne-Vigneau	Rabaud-Promis
Suduiraut	Sigalas-Ribaud

Vineyards listed after the Great Growth of Château d'Yquem are rated as First Growths in the 1855 classification.

GERMAN vineyard whites

All the great German wines are white and light, less than 12 per cent in alcohol, and taste best with all kinds of fish and sea food, with ham and pork, with cold cuts and spicy dishes. They are easy to buy. The German custom of compounding names is confusing in the beginning, but the system of labeling is simple, though detailed.

The key is that the center of the label contains the name of the town, followed by the vineyard from which the wine comes: A wine from the Rheinpfalz vineyard of Jesuitengarten in the town of Forst, for instance, will be called on the label "Forster Jesuitengarten," just as an inhabitant of New York is called a New Yorker. The name of the grower will be shown conspicuously on the label, and the degree of sweetness of the wine will be shown under the vineyard name.

In any good year the owner of a good vineyard will try to make several wines, ranging from dry and flowery to sweet and fruity.

When the grapes contain enough sugar to make a *naturwein,* picking will begin. This wine will not be sweet, except for the floweriness or fruitiness that comes from the alcohols and other constituents of the wine. To distinguish them from the often good but lesser, sugared wines, the grower will add to the label words meaning "natural" or "genuine," those signifying estate-bottling, and those identifying the wine as coming from a particular vineyard, or growth:

142

NATURAL	ESTATE-BOTTLING	GROWTH
Natur	Original-Abfüllung	Wachstum
Naturrein	Kellerabfüllung	Crescenz
Naturwein	Kellerabzug	Gewachs
Echt	Schlossabzug	

The words *echt* and *rein* mean genuine, Abzug and Abfüllung mean bottling, *Keller* means cellar, and *Schloss* means castle. In good years different casks may be bottled separately, the best being called *Kabinett,* or bearing the cask number, *Fass* or *Fuder* in German. These cabinet wines, so called because they were once the wines reserved for the owner in a special cabinet in the cellar, and those bearing cask numbers, are always unsugared wines. Such names are sprinkled on a label like raisins in a good bread pudding, so that they can't be missed. The vineyard name and the grower's are usually enough to identify an unsugared wine. The vintners just want to be sure.

Particularly good bunches of grapes will be left on the vines so that the noble mold, here called *Edelfäule,* will develop. The resulting wine will be quite flowery, with a light and pleasing fruity taste that is almost sweet. Such a wine is called *Spätlese,* meaning late-picked. It is a perfect wine with simply cooked fish and sea food, with ham and other spicy foods. It will probably cost over three dollars a bottle.

Certain bunches of these overripe grapes will show a lot of the noble mold on the grapeskins, and these bunches will be set apart and made separately into a fruity, somewhat sweet wine. It will be called *Auslese,* meaning selection, may cost four dollars and more a bottle, and will taste good with ham, spicy dishes, dishes with a rich or sweet sauce, and with fish and sea food dishes. Sometimes individual grapes showing much *Edelfäule* will be separated for making into wine and, even more rarely, completely shriveled grapes will be set aside. Wines from these are called *Beerenauslese* and *Trockenbeerenauslese*. They are always sweet, rare, and costly, and are drunk by themselves, as a treat, or with sweet, rich foods and desserts. Good ones invariably cost four dollars a bottle and on up to ten and twenty dollars, and are not for everyday drinking. They are the most distinguished of white wines, and the taste is unforgettable.

Most of us are satisfied with Naturwein and Spätlese, however, with an occasional Auslese now and then. Some people think that a grower who uses most of his grapes to make the sweet wines may be depriving the drier wines of many good bunches of grapes. For this reason good vintners sharply limit the amount of Auslesen they make, so that the dry wines from their vineyards will also be of high quality.

Listed here are the most important townships of each of the great German regions, and the outstanding vineyards in each. Wines come from other towns, good wines, and each township will have several more good vineyards. The following lists include the best, the biggest, or the most easily available wines, and set the pattern for those from neighboring vineyards.

SAMPLE MIXED CASE
GERMAN VINEYARD WHITES

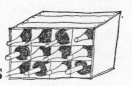

Forster   Rauenthaler
Deidesheimer   Hallgartener
Wachenheimer   Rüdesheimer
Nackenheimer   Zeltinger
Niersteiner   Graacher
Oppenheimer   Wehlener

VINTAGES: Estate-bottlings from these townships are usually on the market within two years of the vintage, and while the sweet wines, the Auslesen, can live for ten years and longer, the drier Spätlesen, from overripe grapes, are often past their prime at seven years or so, as is the Naturwein. These last two are the kinds most often drunk with meals, the Auslesen being drunk by itself or with desserts.

FOODS: The drier wines are wonderful with fish and sea food of all sorts, and with ham and other salty or spicy foods that are somewhat light.

SERVING: These wines should be cooled, but not be served so cold that their floweriness is blunted, an hour in the refrigerator or fifteen minutes in an ice bucket being enough. They are perfect luncheon wines, to be served with light and simple foods, hot or cold.

THE RHEINPFALZ

FORST	**RUPPERTSBERG**
Jesuitengarten	Gaisböhl
Kirchenstück	Spiess
DEIDESHEIM	**KÖNIGSBACH**
Hohenmorgen	**BAD DURKHEIM**
Leinhöhle	**UNGSTEIN**
WACHENHEIM	**KALLSTADT**
Goldbächel	
Gerümpel	

All the great wines of the Pfalz come from a single range of hills in the Mittel-Haardt, the central section of the region, which runs from just south of Ruppertsberg to Wachenheim. The best come from *Deidesheim* and *Forst*,

The phrase above the cask number means the vineyard is owned entirely by a single grower.

Originalabfüllung   Dr. Bürklin-Wolf

Wachenheim an der Weinstraße
RHEINPFALZ

Forster Kirchenstück
Riesling Spätlese

This estate-bottling from late-picked Riesling grapes from the Kirchenstück vineyard in Forst, is bottled by the owner in his main winery at Wachenheim.

the latter township boasting the two most precious pieces of vineyard land in Germany, Jesuitengarten and Kirchenstück. The four neighboring towns listed are generally considered to produce wines of distinction, and good wines come from some of the others. The full, fruity wines from the Riesling vineyards are in the minority, though, for most of the secondary vineyards are planted in Sylvaner. A vineyard name along with that of the town is assurance of a fine bottle. The wines from selected grapes, the Auslesen, may cost five dollars and more.

147

THE RHEINHESSEN

NACKENHEIM
  Rothenberg
  Engelsberg
NIERSTEIN
  Rehbach
  Hipping
OPPENHEIM
  Kreuz
  Sackträger

BINGEN
  Scharlachberg
  Ohligberg
BODENHEIM
DIENHEIM
WORMS

The best vineyards of the Rheinhessen are planted in Riesling, and the labels carefully note the fact.

There are two main centers of fine vineyards in Hessia: in the township of *Nackenheim* and its neighbors, *Nierstein* and *Oppenheim;* and near *Bingen*, at the mouth of the Nahe. Bingen's neighbors, Büdesheim and Kempten, put their names on labels along with that of Bingen, plus a vineyard, so you get such jawbreakers as Binger-Büdesheimer Schnackenberg. There's no need for dismay, though, for the principle of a town name plus a vineyard is still the basic way of identifying a good wine. Nackenheimers are the German favorites, although Niersteiners are better known abroad. The Nackenheimers are famous for great balance and lightness. The three other towns listed also can produce good wines. Most of the Hessian vineyards are planted in Sylvaner, and most of the Hessian wines go to market under the regional name of "Liebfraumilch," which can be good or bad, but which is usually only ordinary.

THE NAHE

SCHLOSS BÖCKELHEIM	NORHEIM
KREUZNACH	MUNSTER
NIEDERHAUSEN	ROXHEIM

The Nahe empties into the Rhine at Bingen, and if its vineyards weren't on its own river slopes, they would probably be grouped with the Rheinhessen. They have their own character, however, and wines from the towns listed above have an increasing reputation in Germany. Many of the vineyards have been planted or reconstituted in the past decade or so, and will begin making their names known on the international markets in the next few years.

149

THE RHEINGAU

HOCHHEIM
Domdechaney
Kirchenstück
ELTVILLE
Sonnenberg
Langenstück
RAUENTHAL
Baiken
Gehrn
KIEDRICH
Gräfenberg
Wasserrose
ERBACH
Marcobrunn
Siegelsberg
HATTENHEIM
Steinberg
Wisselbrunnen

OESTRICH
Lenchen
Doosberg
HALLGARTEN
Schönhell
Deutelsberg
WINKEL
Schloss Vollrads
Hasensprung
JOHANNISBERG
Schloss Johannisberg
Klaus
GEISENHEIM
Rothenberg
Klauserweg
RUDESHEIM
Berg Rottland
Berg Roseneck

A single range of hills five miles long forms Germany's greatest district. The dozen towns of the Rheingau are along the river and back in the hills, sweep after sweep of vineyard. They begin near *Hochheim,* which gives the English nickname of "hocks" to the big, fruity, superbly balanced white wines. The lesser wines of the town are poor, but those from the top dozen vineyards are soft and full.

The *Eltvillers* come from numerous vineyards, and because they are not well known abroad, they are among the best buys of all German wines, unless restaurants and shops jack their prices to snatch profits. A good

This estate-bottling was actually bottled at the producer's main winery in Eltville.

merchant or restaurateur with sense enough to buy these wines ought to have sense enough to price them well below the famous Johannisbergers and Hattenheimers, just as he should do with the Fixins of Burgundy or the fourth- and fifth-classed growths of Bordeaux. The wines are big and full and soft.

The *Erbachers,* from neighboring downstream vineyards, are hard in comparison to Eltvillers, and consequently long-lived. The outstanding vineyard, the Marcobrunner, is on the town boundary toward Hattenheim, and its fruity wine is so outstanding that it often goes to market without the town name.

The *Hattenheimers* are like the Marcobrunners, in being full and balanced, its supreme vineyard being the Steinberg, back in the hills, whose *Auslesen* and *Spätlesen* are always among top rank.

Also back in the hills are the wines of *Rauenthal,* which are the German favorites and always high-priced, and those of *Kiedrich,* big and fruity like the Rauenthalers, but much lower in price because they are not well known.

The vineyards of *Hallgarten* and *Johannisberg* are also back in the hills, as is the outstanding vineyard of *Winkel,* Schloss Vollrads, which doesn't use the town name to identify its wines. In great years the wines are magnificent and full, but they are often below par in years less than very good. All the wines have great balance. Schloss Johannisberg is probably the most famous of all German wines, because of its great breed.

The *Oestrichers* are soft, and without the distinction of the Hallgarteners they resemble.

VINEYARD WHITES

The *Geisenheimers* and *Rüdesheimers* are wines that excel in fair and good years, and are often out of balance in great years and those that are excessively dry. Those from the Rüdesheimer Berg, a group of vineyards on a single hill, are probably the fullest of the Rheingaus.

THE MOSELLE

ERDEN
  Treppchen
  Prälat
URZIG
  Würzgarten
  Lay
ZELTINGEN
  Himmelreich
  Schlossberg
WEHLEN
  Sonnenuhr
  Nonnenberg

GRAACH
  Josephshof
  Himmelreich
BERNKASTEL
  Doktor
  Lay
BRAUNEBERG
  Juffer
  Falkenberg
PIESPORT
  Goldtröpfchen
  Lay

153

Moselle vineyards begin in the outskirts of Coblenz, on the Rhine, but the best wines come from the steep vineyards above the looping river between Traben-Trarbach and Piesport, the district called the Mittel-Mosel. Before you reach these great vineyards, there is a group of towns with well-known names, producing popular wines, like the Schwarze Katz of Zell and the Nacktarsch of Kröv. Black cats and bare behinds may make novel labels, but the wines have no distinction. The good wines begin at Erden.

Erdeners come from vineyards across the river from the town, adjoining those that produce *Urzigers.* Erdeners seem to be good even in ordinary years, outstanding in great ones, while the Urzigers, which mature slowly, are known for a particularly spicy quality, and are often *spritzig,* or slightly sparkling. The *Auslesen* from Urzig may take five years to reach their prime, a year longer than its neighbors, and a great bottle may still be outstanding a dozen years after the vintage.

The *Zeltingers* come from many vineyards, and a vineyard name on the label is practically a guarantee of an outstanding wine. A wine labeled simply with the town name is no assurance of a fine wine, though, a fact that holds for all the towns of the German districts. The *Wehleners* are like the Zeltingers in being flowery and well balanced, and are today considered to be among the best of the wines from the Moselle.

Graachers are the wines that have most fame today, however, being particularly distinguished by an excellent balance of qualities. The principal vineyard, Josephshof, goes to market as Josephshöfer, without the town name on the label.

The *Bernkastelers* and those from the twin town across the river, Kues, are full and well-made wines, but perhaps overpriced because of the Doktor, the most famous vineyard, whose wines are equaled by several others from the neighboring slopes. All possess a particular taste that the Germans call smoky, although the fullness and floweriness of the wine is what one is most apt to notice.

The *Piesporters* and *Braunebergers*—the first generally light and delicate, the second full, rich and fruity—come from the other two towns that produce outstanding wines. In both cases vineyard names are needed to get the best wines.

A few other towns produce good wines that rarely attain the balance and fineness of those listed above, but bottles from Wintrich, Dhron, and Trittenheim are particularly pleasant to drink when they are not high in price. The Trittenheimers, especially, should be drunk young.

German wines were once the best labeled in the world. They are no longer. Some of the most famous vineyard names are now *Gattungsnamen,* generic names no longer meaning wines from specific vineyards, unless the wines are *original Abfüllung,* estate-bottlings. None are listed here. Equally, new laws state that a town name can be put on any wine within nine miles of the town. These *Gattungsnamen,* generic names, mean that a Piesporter no longer need be a wine of Piesport, and this holds for all the rest of the wine towns. Not so wicked as it sounds, the generic names now stand for blends of wines in substantial quantity and at reasonable prices.

155

THE SAAR

WILTINGEN
  Scharzhofberg
  Braune Kupp
OBEREMMEL
  Hütte
  Rosenberg

AYE
  Kupp
  Herrenberg
OCKFEN
  Bockstein
  Geisberg
KANZEM
NEIDERMENNIG

THE RUWER

MAXIMIN GRUNHAUS
EITELSBACH
KASEL

TRIER

AVELSBACH

Two small tributaries, the Saar and the Ruwer, flow into the Mosel near Trier, and the wines from these vineyards are some of the most unusual in the world. Even in great years they are incredibly light, almost ethereal. They are wines to drink by themselves, during the day or late at night, when one's mood is light as the wine and there is time for frivolity. They are holiday wines, somehow, for drinking when the cares of the world are far away, or one wishes they could be—the wines to drink when Champagne would be too heady and not thirst-quenching enough. They should always be drunk young, and are at their best only in the good and great vintages, being too light and acid in years that are only fair.

Vineyard names are necessary to insure a good wine, even in a minor town like Kasel.

NOTE: There are many other vineyards in each township, and when the wines are bottled by the owner they are generally good buys.

AUSTRIA

Most Austrian wines are drunk within her borders, much of it in Vienna itself, which boasts the suburb of Grinzing, where young *Heurige*, the most popular of Austrian white wines, is made. The best wines come from Vöslau and Loiben, Krems and Durnstein, with others from Gumpoldskirchen, the latter being the one most often found outside the country. Made from the Riesling, these wines are light but intense, without heaviness. Someday more of them may be available on this market.

TOKAY

Tokay comes from a small wine district near the Hungarian village of Tokaj. It is made from a grape called the Furmint, and the wine is the most tonic of all wines, bottles a century old often being found to be in perfect condition. Overripe grapes are picked and pressed, and to the juice is added the oozings from 30-pound baskets, called *puttonyos,* full of grapes attacked by the noble rot. The number of baskets of juice added is a gauge of the sweetness and quality of the wine. The resulting wine is called *Aszu,* while the oozings from the baskets, when fermented separately, are called *Eszencia. Szamorodni* Tokay is made by using fully ripe grapes along with overripe ones and those that have raisinized.

Aszu and Eszencia are too intensely sweet and full for any but the rarest occasions, but Szamorodni is an excellent wine to drink instead of, or with, a light dessert. It is supposed to have a bouquet like that of fresh bread.

Hungary produces a variety of excellent white wines from Riesling and Furmint grapes, and a group of superior red wines from districts near Lake Balaton, but these are rarely seen on the American market.

Pink Wines

Pink wines are the easiest to buy and serve, and the sight of a bottle on a shelf or cooling in a bucket is almost a relief to anybody who is still fretting about reading labels and can't yet believe that serving red wines or whites is as easy as experts say. After all, books are written about wines, and while it's well and good to claim that a book and its lists are useful to steer bibbers to good wines and away from poor ones, the existence of a book shows a certain complexity and a sizable amount of information. Pink wines make it possible to drink without reading anything, not even a label, because they are generally good no matter where they come from, rarely cost much over three dollars a bottle, and can be found in just about every wineshop and good restaurant in the land. The joys of drinking them may not be as satisfying or exciting as those that attend the drinking of red and white wines, but the pinks are cool, refreshing, and cheerful, possessed of wine's basic virtue of making a meal festive. Pink wines are a relief, just the ones to serve when unknowledgeable guests might think a grander wine is a sign of putting on the dog. Nobody is apt to think a pink wine is pretentious.

The only trouble with pink wine is its name, because "pink" generally connotes the delicate and feminine. Pink wines are usually heady and full of taste, and are feminine only in that they are beguiling, hiding under a fruity and easy-to-drink freshness an alcoholic strength of 12 per cent or so. Fairly full and robust, they go particularly well with spicy and well-seasoned dishes, with hearty stews and casseroles, with cold cuts and delicatessen, with fish or sea food served with a sauce. They always taste best chilled, and hostesses love them because they are the wines to serve when there are doubts about what's right. Like Champagne, a pink wine is an all-purpose wine, and much cheaper than the bubbly.

The best of them come from France, where they are called *rosés*, which has a pleasanter sound than "pink," and where they are usually served with lunch. Every wine district produces them, but the favorites come from the Rhone district of Tavel; from Arbois in the Savoy; and from the Loire district of Anjou. In Tavel, the Grenache Rosé grape is used, and this grape produces good pink wines wherever it is planted. Some of the Tavels are almost red, and are always a true pink in color, no matter how deep in hue. They are made by pressing the red grapes, then removing the juice from the skins, so that only a part of the color is picked up by the fermenting wine. Very close to them in character, although lighter and less fruity, are the pink wines of Provence, made in Riviera vineyards on the coast and back in the hills. The best Provence rosés usually go to market under vineyard names, under the general appellation "Côtes de Provence," the vineyard name usually being preceded by the word "Domaine" or "Clos." The word "Château" is sometimes used. Vineyard names also appear on bottles of Tavel, and generally indicate a superior wine. The list of outstanding French rosés is small.

FRENCH ROSÉS
  Tavel
  Rosé d'Arbois
  Rosé d'Anjou
  Côtes de Provence

Even the shippers in Bordeaux and Burgundy now produce some pink wines, and others come from the Maury and Banyuls districts near the Pyrenees, but these last are often sweet. Alsace shippers market a rosé they call "vin gris," made from wines brought into the district, but these are generally low in quality.

Pink wines are made in Italy's northern districts, but they are rarely shipped abroad. There is little point when such excellent pink wines are made in California, the best of which is invariably marketed under the grape name, Grenache Rosé.

All pink wines taste best when young, improving only slightly, if at all, in the bottle. They are at their best when under two years old, and well chilled.

Champagne and
Sparkling Wines

Champagne is one of the great wines of the world, and no other sparkling wines can compare, although every wine district in the world tries hard. The Champagne vineyards are north of Burgundy and east of Paris, centered around the small villages of Ay and Épernay, although many wines are stored in the miles of caverns beneath the city of Reims. Champagne is produced solely from the Pinot grapes of Burgundy, the Pinot Noir being planted along the banks of the Marne and on the flanks of the Montagne de Reims, which lies just to the south of that cathedral city, while the Pinot Blanc is planted along a ridge of hills called the Côte des Blancs, which extends south from the town of Épernay. The wines take six years and longer to be prepared for market, which accounts for part of the high cost, but the main reason Champagne is so expensive is that it is so heavily taxed.

Most Champagne is made from a blend of black and white grapes which are pressed quickly, the juice being poured into large vats for fermenting, away from the skins, which would color the juice. Such a blend is called a *cuvée*. After the fermentation is complete, the wines are put in bottles with a dosage of sugar added. After they are laid on their sides in the cellars, a second fermentation takes place in the bottles, as the added sugar is converted into alcohol and carbon dioxide. The fermentation is slow, taking place each spring and fall, when the vines flower in the vineyard and when the vintage is made. The bottles rest in the changeless temperature of the cellars for several years, sometimes five or six, depositing a heavy sediment.

When the wine is ready, the bottles are shaken and their necks stuck in slanting racks. Each day for a couple of months the bottle is shaken and tipped slightly, so that the sediment gradually works its way to the neck and the bottle stands on end. When the sediment is solidly against the cork, a deft workman carefully pulls the cork, the pressure of gas shoots out the plug of the sediment, and the bottle is quickly filled with wine from the same lot and corked again. After a few months the wine has recovered from the shock of the disgorging and is ready to be drunk. The process has taken at least half a dozen years, but the wine will continue to improve for another three or four, then stay at its prime for several years longer; great vintages are often excellent twenty years later.

When the wines are originally blended in the vats, those from the black-grape vineyards are balanced by the lighter and more delicate wines from the white-grape vineyards. In the same way wines from one vintage will be balanced with those from another, for it is rare that a single vintage will have all the qualities of a fine Champagne. In exceptional years, vintage Champagnes are made, but they are rarely worth the extra price demanded for them.

When the sediment is disgorged, a dosage of sugar is added to sweeten the wine. It is fashionable today to drink only the driest Champagne, the type called *Brut*, but Brut must be made from the very best wines or it will taste too dry and hard. The type called "Extra Sec" is generally the one most widely produced, and therefore more reasonable in price and more readily available. These two are the Champagnes that taste best by themselves, or with hors d'oeuvres or a cold buffet. *Sec* tastes full and fruity, generally, and sometimes slightly sweet, so it is the Champagne most generally served with meals, when Extra Dry would be too dry. Some sweet Champagnes are still made, principally for the South American market, but these are too sweet for most tastes, even when served with desserts. The following percentages indicate how much sugar syrup is added, at the time of the disgorging, to sweeten the Champagnes.

> Brut—less than 1 per cent sugar dissolved in wine
> Extra Sec—less than 2 per cent
> Sec—over 3 per cent but less than 6 per cent
> Demi-sec—up to 8 per cent
> Doux—10 per cent or more

Some Champagne is made only from the white wines produced from the Côte des Blancs, and this is considered to be the finest and most delicate of all Champagnes. It is called "white of whites," *Blanc de Blancs,* and is often sold by the name of the township from which it comes. The vineyards of the various townships are rated on a sliding scale, and are priced accordingly. The towns of Mesnil, Avize, and Cramant, for instance, being rated 100 per cent, are considered to produce the finest Blanc de Blancs.

Champagnes are known by brands, and some twenty top houses ship their wines to the United States, along with a host of smaller, but often good, producers. Full-bodied Champagnes, like those from Krug, Bollinger, Charles Heidsieck, Perrier-Jouet, and Dom Perignon of Moët & Chandon, are preferred by some experts, although the generally lighter and more delicate Champagnes like Veuve Clicquot, Taittinger, and Piper-Heidsieck are doted on by many Champagne lovers. Here's a list of some of the leading houses.

Ayala	Besserat de Bellefon
Bollinger	Château Salon
Heidsieck Monopole	Charles Heidsieck
Krug	Irroy
Moët & Chandon	Lanson
Mercier	Mumm
Piper-Heidsieck	Perrier-Jouet
Pommery & Greno	Pol Roger
St. Marceaux	Louis Roederer
Taittinger	Veuve-Clicquot-Ponsardin

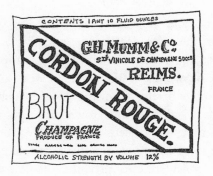

This house is the largest shipper of Champagne.

Producers generally hold new vintages off the market until the preceding vintage has been sold, and we are

166

now working on the quick-to-mature '62s, elegant and balanced, and the even greater '61s. The full '64s and softer, rounder '66s will occupy us until the middle of the decade, and we can only hope for a great vintage early in the seventies. The highly touted '59s turned out to be heavy wines with little elegance, making the demand strong for the good and great wines of the sixties. General prosperity increases the pressure, and prices will go up and up, as it is now doing for all great wines. A wise buyer will lay in as much wine as possible now, for drinking at the decade's turn.

The only trouble with Champagne is its price, with good ones beginning at over eight dollars for non-vintage wines. Vintage Champagnes cost another two dollars a bottle. Consequently, there's plenty of room on the market for lesser sparkling wines at lower prices, but the tax is so high that even American sparkling wines of good quality cost over four dollars a bottle, and the imports cost more. You can't win.

Champagnes aren't simply white wines with bubbles, for the wines are magically transmuted into something much more than that. All other sparkling wines taste like wines with bubbles added, even the pink Champagnes that are made by leaving the wine with the skins for a time. But the classic white Champagnes are a bubbly essence, and have a special foamy quality in the mouth that is inseparable from the taste of the wine. It is hard to describe the difference but easy to taste, and makes of Champagne a wine that is unique.

Every French district produces sparkling wines, and

167

those most like Champagne in possessing this unity of taste, in wine and bubbles combined, are the dry sparkling wines from the Savoy. They are beginning to come on this market. Sparkling wines of excellent quality, but often quite sweet, are produced in the Loire districts of Vouvray and Saumur. All the other French sparkling wines are mediocre, although sparkling Burgundy, made from lesser red wines of that region, is popular outside France, and often palatable. Because of the high taxes on sparkling wines, the same for Champagne as for the others, the lesser wines are overpriced, even when pleasant to drink.

The same is true of the sparkling wines of Italy, the best-known of which are *Lacryma Christi* and *Asti Spumante*. Sparkling wines from Germany and the other countries of Europe rarely come up to the Italian level, the possible exception being a pink crackling wine from Portugal, *Lancer's,* which has a few bubbles.

Things are much brighter when you look at sparkling wines made in New York and California. They are usually well-balanced wines, properly dry and extremely well made. Those from New York are particularly distinguished, employing in their blends wines made from native American grapes and from hybrids. California uses the classic French Pinot grapes and other European varieties to produce some particularly full-bodied and well-balanced wines. Here are some of the brands of consistently good sparkling wines.

NEW YORK	CALIFORNIA	
Gold Seal	Beaulieu	Schramsberg
Widmer's	Christian Brothers	Korbel
Great Western	Hanns Kornell	Almadén
Taylor	Charles Krug	Paul Masson
		Weibel

The American vintners listed above follow the Champagne method of producing sparkling wines, by having the second fermentation take place in the bottle. Sparkling wines are also produced in bulk by having the second fermentation take place in large vats, then bottling the wine under pressure. This produces a wine with large bubbles, and there is little union between the wine and its sparkle. Only a wine that is bottle-fermented will produce the fine bubble, called a bead, that is the sign of a good sparkling wine. A still cheaper method is to carbonate still wines by pumping gas into them, and these are even poorer than bulk-fermented wines. Both bulk-fermented and carbonated wines carry the same sparkling-wine tax as the bottle-fermented wines, which makes them exorbitant at any price.

If a wine is bottled too soon after the initial fermentation, or if there is some sugar that has not been converted to alcohol, the wines are apt to continue fermenting after bottling and will show a slight sparkle. This is often quite pleasing. Wines of the Loire are apt to show this quality, which the French call *pétillant,* which means prickling. The Germans call it *spritzig.* This slight sparkle is quite common in Swiss wines, where it is referred to as the "star" in the wine. The normally still wines seem to twinkle in the glass, and have a particularly sprightly taste.

The French call all sparkling wines *vins mousseux,* frothy or foaming wines; the Italians call them *spumante* —and all of them wish the sparkling wines were Champagne. But the only Champagnes come from the 22,000 acres of vineyard in the Champagne district, the only place on earth where the truly great sparkling wines are

169

made. Champagnes are expensive and are overly taxed, but most people feel that the glorious wines mean joy and celebration and are worth the cost. Champagnes are the most universally liked of all wines. None deserves fame more.

Aromatic Wines

Wine was hot and rough in the old days. This is always a pleasure to report because the superiority of things ancient is so often touted to show the poverty of our times. Few ancient wines could be drunk without doctoring, and drinking the Mediterranean vintages straight was looked upon as depravity, not so much moral but more as showing a gluttonous stupidity. The feverish wines were mingled with water, or cooled by trickling them through strainers full of snow. Their harshness was softened by sweetening them with honey. Tingling spices and flowery herbs were steeped in them to mask their coarseness. The same devices have been used ever since, to correct deficiencies in wine or to improve or enhance the natural vintages, and these are the wines we class today as aromatics. They are some of the most pleasing wines of the modern world and are, of course, far better than anything the ancients knew.

Americans are used to drinking soda pop, beer, and hard stuff, and to widen this rigid pattern means going through a change of life. Drinking wines and such seems part of a gentle life, out of keeping with the robust pioneer spirit that has made our country great—something for the soft and citified, not for the fun-loving, sporty sort that works hard and plays harder, in and out of the club. Travel removes some of the doubts from which this at-

171

titude stems, and simple curiosity can overcome timidity about the unknown. The number of those who couple strong drink with lustiness and wine with winsomeness is decreasing among us, and even the burliest of the pinnacle climbers are now enjoying the gregarious delights of all things potable, with scarcely a twinge as to whether their manliness is being questioned when they swig something that isn't fizzy, malty, or 86 proof. Willy-nilly, wines are winning a proper place in American life.

We are used to jolts, quenching, and sweetness in our drinks. The definite tastes of wines, with the easy lift of spirits that comes from drinking them, take some getting used to. Wines don't quench thirst the way that beer or soft drinks do, because wines are drunk in smaller quantities. And sweetness is not the only taste in wine. The desire for something to drink is satisfied, by wines, in affecting the other kinds of taste buds in the mouth, primarily those that register bitter and sour. Enjoyment depends on familiarity; it is hard to feel expectancy or anticipation for what is unfamiliar. The satisfaction that comes from new sensations must be known before they can be desired.

All of which depends on a pleasant learning process, and the aromatic wines, which the French call *apéritifs* and the Italians *aperitívos,* are particularly rewarding. There are not many of them, and they are invariably drunk between meals, chilled or with ice, and with or without soda. They taste strange, at first, and mild, because we are used to cocktails and highballs. But if one of them is drunk at cocktail time, say, once a week for a month or so, the drinker finds that it is a good change from "the usual."

172

One begins to hanker for them now and then, particularly when a heavy meal or a strenuous activity is in the offing.

There are two main kinds of aromatic wines: those that taste of quinine; and vermouth, which tastes of wormwood. All are made by steeping herbs and spices in wine. The wine is invariably one that is strongly acid in taste, and it is made that way on purpose. The acid taste is counteracted by the herbs and spices, or by adding sweetness. Most aromatic wines are brought up to the strength of fortified wines—between 14 per cent and 21 per cent alcohol—by the addition of brandy. At an average strength of 16 per cent or 18 per cent, the various tastes of the wines, seasonings, and brandy can be stabilized, so that the aromatic wine that results will be consistent in taste from year to year.

Vermouth is an ancient drink, but the modern industry was established in Turin, in the Italian Piedmont, in the eighteenth century. The desire was to devise a uniform product from the many wines of the Piedmont. At first red wines were used, and these were heavily sweetened, so that Italian Vermouth came to be considered a sweet Vermouth. The French had an excess of white wines from southern vineyards in the nineteenth century, so the vintners of Marseilles developed a dry Vermouth, which became famous. Today every wine country makes both sweet and dry Vermouths, but the best still come from Italy and France. They taste best chilled, with an ice cube or two added, along with a twist of lemon. The basic taste is still of wormwood, but over twenty seasonings are used in making the blends. The color comes from these seasonings, and from aging in casks, but the pointless current fashion for Vermouths light in color requires that they be bleached or filtered, which removes much of their taste.

A special kind of Vermouth with a pronounced quinine taste is bitter Vermouth, primarily made in Italy. This is often drunk with ice, but tastes better when served with soda or mixed half and half with a regular Vermouth, the highball glass then being filled with soda.

Just as Vermouth came to mean Italy, so did the bitter-sweet tonic taste of quinine-based aromatic wines come to mean France, and sidewalk cafés would not be the same without these apéritifs. Usually they are made from red wines, but white wines are used for some, and other herbs, barks, and spices are added to vary the taste. Today every wine country produces them, and some of the most distinguished come from Spain. Based on Sherry, the Spanish group is known collectively as *Jerez Quina,* and they are among the most intense of the world's aromatic wines.

But it is the French apéritifs that set the pattern, and most of them are excellent. Drunk with ice and soda, they are an alcoholic Gallic version of our soda pop, but they seem to taste best when served chilled, with ice and perhaps a twist of lemon. The best-known and most easily obtainable are the following, all of which have a pronounced taste of quinine:

FRENCH APÉRITIFS
  Byrrh
  Dubonnet
  Lillet
  Pikina
  Roc
  St. Raphaël

Bitters themselves are extracts of herbs, roots, and so forth to which spirits and sweetening are added to make a concentrated flavoring. Anywhere from a dash to a jigger or so can be added to give tang to a drink—a Vermouth and soda, for instance. Like Vermouths, they are known by brand names, and each has its distinctive taste.

There is an endless list of Vermouths and bitters, but those listed are the best-known.

ITALIAN VERMOUTH
Carpano
Cinzano
Cora
Gancia
Martini & Rossi
Stock

FRENCH VERMOUTH
Boissière
Cazalis & Prat
Chambéry
Dolin
Noilly Prat

BITTER VERMOUTH
Campari
Carpano Punt e Mes
Freund Ballor
Ferretti soda

BITTERS
Amara
Angostura
Boonekamp
Calysia
Fernet Branca
Peychauds
Secrestat

There are several Italian aromatic wines with pronounced quinine tastes, perhaps the best being the one made from the red wine of Barolo, called Barolo Chinato. But much more interesting are the Marsala wines, which are flavored not only with the various aromatics but also with eggs, almonds, hazelnuts, coffee, chocolate, and other things. This is the soda-fountain approach to making apéritifs, Italian-style, and what's amazing is that the results are interesting to drink. Practically everything has been used in apéritifs at one time or another, leading some people to believe that the producers are today's version of medieval alchemists. One of the oddest, which has some reputation in Italy, is Cynar, which has an artichoke base.

Northern Europe goes in for doctoring up spirits to make all kinds of liqueurs, but Germany produces one aromatic wine that is a tradition as well as a drink. That's *Maiwein,* which is the newly made white wine from the previous vintage, in which sprays of *waldmeister,* the spicy herb we call woodruff, have been steeped. It's traditional to float the new wild strawberries in bowls of the scented wine to celebrate the first coming of spring, but today May Wine is shipped all over the world, to be drunk any time of the year. It's best in the spring, when you make it yourself by adding the herb to a bottle of your favorite German regional.

Wines sweetened with sugar syrup, but without aromatics, are generally lumped as "kosher wines" in American shops. Red or white, they usually taste like grape juice, and even though wines compose the basic liquid content, they belong to the class of alcoholic fruit drinks. Fermentations of other fruits are called wines, those from pears being called "perry," for instance. Those from honey are called "mead" or "metheglin." All kinds of fruits and berries are fermented in northern Europe, and the best of these is generally considered to be the cherry wine of the Scandinavian countries. This can be pleasant to drink as an apéritif, or as a mild after-dinner drink, and generally tastes best chilled. But wine is basically the fermented juice of freshly squeezed grapes, and anything else is a poor relation.

There are dozens of other aromatic wines, made all over the world, but those of France and Italy stand out and are most readily available. We have begun making our own, appropriately calling them by American names, such as Thunderbird, Silver Satin, Golden Spur, Ripple, and who knows how many others? None has any distinction, being generally bland and insipid in taste. But there's no reason at all why a spiked soft drink that tastes good can't be made in this country, and a flood of well-made American aromatic wines is due to gush out of California or New York State any day now. As it is, several of the great European aromatic wines are now made here, using European flavoring extracts and formulas to reproduce the foreign tastes, with American wines as a base. And it's not easy to spot the difference, except that the American versions seem to have less taste and intensity. The Californians are busy trying to outdo the Europeans, steeping, infusing, macerating, and advertising as never before, and in no time at all the only manly thing to do will be to drink an aromatic wine with a pleasing taste and an even more pleasing name. Until they come along, though, there are the aromatic wines of Europe to quench our thirsts and satisfy our cravings when a cocktail or highball won't quite hit the spot.

Fortified Wines

SPANISH SHERRY

Chaucer noted that Sherry was a "wyn . . . that when a man hath drinken draughtes three . . . he is in Spayne." This ability to transport the drinker to foreign places is a quality common to fortified wines particularly. The trade description, that they are blended wines brought to between 14 per cent and 21 per cent with brandy so that they are poised at certain characteristic tastes, scarcely hints at their volatile and intense natures. They are closest to what a man who has no familiarity with wine imagines a wine should be. Three of them—Spanish Sherry, Portuguese Port, and Madeira—can possess great distinction and are classed as great wines, along with the best table wines and sparkling wines from the regions of Bordeaux, Burgundy, Champagne, the Rhine, and Tokay.

All true Sherry comes from a region of some 20,000 acres near Jerez, up the Atlantic coast from Gibraltar. It is about the size of the island of Manhattan, and boasts a particularly chalky soil called *albariza,* in which is planted the white Palomino grape—the two natural elements, along with the climate, needed to produce these great wines. The method of blending, called the *solera* system (meaning foundation), is man's contribution. A *solera* consists of tiers of casks, usually three. Wine for shipment is drawn from the tier of the *solera* containing the oldest wines; this row of casks is refilled from the tier containing the next oldest wines, which is refilled, in turn, from the youngest tier of the *solera*. The youngest tier is replenished with year-old wines from a separate group of casks called the *criadera*, meaning cradle or crib. Like everything else to do with Spanish Sherry, the *solera* system is controlled by law and custom, so that no more than half the wine is withdrawn from the oldest tier of a *solera* in any one year. At least two years are needed, then, for a wine to pass from one tier to the next, and as the wine is already at least a year old when it is put in the *solera*, the youngest Sherries available on the market are at least seven years old. The wines are usually much older, the draw from a *solera* being so slow that a wine may take five years, or ten, to pass from one tier to the next.

The reason for the system is that young wines take on the characteristics of the older wines in the *solera*—they are "educated to the *solera*," vintners say—and since most *soleras* go back to the early nineteenth century and many of them consist of a thousand casks and more, large quantities of young wine are made homogeneous with old stocks. Vintners like to say that there is in every draw a trace of the wines originally laid down, but there is nothing at all fanciful about the fact that the young Sherries quickly take on the characteristics of the old wines in the *solera*.

The system is essential to Sherry because new wines vary so widely. Two casks of juice, fermenting side by side, made from grapes of the same vineyard, and pressed at the same time, can produce quite different wines. When the wines are tasted the spring after the vintage, they are matched to the various *soleras*, and wines that cannot

179

be matched are made into brandy or rejected. Gradations are endless, in practice being reduced to the dozen or more *soleras* operated by a shipping firm.

Basically there are only two kinds of Sherry. A *Fino* results when a film of yeast called the *flor,* or flower, develops on the surface of the new wine. These are light, pungent, highly volatile wines that round out in seven years, and are the Spanish favorites for everyday drinking. Some of the Finos will be heavy and rough in the beginning, and need ten years or more to develop; these acquire a pleasingly nutty taste after ten years in cask, and are called *Amontillados. Finos* aged in bodegas on the coast, in the town of Sanlúcar, develop a tonic, almost salty, dryness that is said to come from the sea breezes. These are called *Manzanillas.* They mature in seven years, are hard to find outside of Spain, and are the driest wines in the world.

A type called *Oloroso* results when no *flor* forms on the wine. The youngest need a decade or longer to develop and, like all Sherries, continue to become more intense with age. Old, and expensive, sweetening wines are added to these Olorosos to produce the sweetened Sherries that are drunk outside of Spain. These are called Cream, Brown, or East India Sherries. A lightly sweetened Oloroso is sometimes dubbed Amoroso, a name the English seem to like because it suggests the nature of this wine of passion without really saying so. A famous example is "Dry Sack," shipped by Williams & Humbert.

The Spanish prefer their Sherries dry, including the Olorosos, drinking them as they come from the bottle or cool from the cellar or chilled, any time of the day or night, with or without food.

Victorian England had so many wines coming in from Europe that it became necessary to set up rules for drinking them, and Sherry was relegated to the time just before meals. Sherries taste fine then, but they also taste good with salty, spicy, or highly seasoned foods. They are traditionally served with the soup course at formal dinners, but they also go well with fowl and fish and seafood courses, particularly those served with sauces.

Cooking Sherry originally was merely the bottle reserved for use in the kitchen, being part of the regular supply used for drinking. After Prohibition the grocery lobby saw to it that a regulation was passed permitting the sale in groceries of wines called "cooking Sherry," the proviso being that it be loaded with salt so that it was unfit to drink. Practically any wine is used for this, and all it does for a dish is to load it with salt. Real sherries are the best wines for cooking. Being intense in taste, they should be use sparingly, so that their abilities to blend and bring out flavors can be employed. When more than a few tablespoonfuls are needed, the wines are generally mixed half and half with water. No wine is more imitated, but the imitations bear little resemblance to the Sherries of Spain.

Spanish Sherry is about the only wine that does not deteriorate quickly once the cork is pulled, the reason being that Sherry develops in the presence of air, whereas other wines fade. Perhaps that is why the English called it the wine of welcome, because a bottle was always

181

ready to serve the arriving guest. Perhaps the instant readiness of Sherry is also why it occupies such a central position in English social life, it being easy to bridge an awkward pause with, "Won't you have a glass of Sherry?"

MANZANILLA

Very dry, with a salty tang. Serve chilled, as an apéritif, and with all kinds of fish and sea food and dishes with a spicy or salty savor.

La Gitana—*Hidalgo*
Manzanilla Superior—*Pedro Domecq*

FINO

Very dry. Serve chilled, on the rocks, or as it comes from the bottle, as a cocktail, or with soups, fish, fowl, ham, spicy foods.

Victoria—Bobadilla
Pinta—Duff Gordon
Fino San Patricio—Garvey & Co.
Tio Pepe—Gonzalez Byass
Bristol Dry—Harvey's
Pale Dry—Palomino
La Ina—Pedro Domecq
Apitiv—Sandeman
Huntington—Valdespino
Bone Dry—Williams & Humbert

AMONTILLADO

Nutty, medium-dry. Serve on the rocks, chilled, or as it comes from the bottle, as a cocktail, or with soup, stews, roasts, dishes with sauces.

Duff Gordon Amontillado
Garvey's Amontillado
Nectar Amontillado—
  Gonzalez Byass
Harvey's Amontillado

Palomino Amontillado
Amontillado Primero—
  Pedro Domecq
Sandeman Amontillado

OLOROSO

Full, rich. Serve on the rocks, chilled, or as it comes from the bottle, during the day with cakes and pastry, with dishes with sweet savor or a cream sauce, and with all sorts of desserts.

Bobadilla Cream
Duff Gordon Cream
Colony Cream—Garvey & Co.
Crema—Gonzalez Byass
Bristol Cream—Harvey's
Palomino Cream
Renfield Cream

Celebration Cream—
  Pedro Domecq
Armada Cream—Sandeman
Cream—Terry's
Carlton House—Valdespino
Canasta Cream—
  Williams & Humbert

PORT

The great red wine of Portugal is named after the northern port of Oporto, although the vineyards are far up the Douro River, which flows into the sea by the hilly city and which separates the lodges where the wine is stored from the place that gave the wine its name. No matter, for the wine goes around the world, its name convincing many that it has named a country, which was named after all its ports, not merely one. To confound imitators, Port from Portugal is now being called Porto.

Port is naturally sweet, its fermentation being stopped by brandy, and it is blended, the full being balanced with the light, the old giving character to the young. When the vintage has been good, shippers may "declare a vintage," bottling the wine after it has been two years in the wood, and shipping it to England. There the wine matures, often for twenty years, until it has developed the compelling bouquet and round, full taste that makes *Vintage Port* one of the best and rarest of tastes in the world of wine. To hasten the maturing, Vintage Ports are sometimes matured in casks for perhaps half a dozen years before bottling, and these *Late-Bottled Ports* are similar to the Vintage Ports, but without their subtleties of taste.

Most commonly, however, Ports mature in butts, called pipes, in the lodges of Vila Nova de Gaia, the town across the Douro from Oporto. Ports from the wood are a deep red after a few years, and are then bottled as *Ruby Port;* they continue to improve for several years after bottling. If the wine is left still longer in the wood, it will become pale in color, and is bottled as *Tawny Port.* Both Ruby and Tawny are blended with wines of their own types to produce the final "styles," each shipping firm's styles being distinctive. Ports long in bottle form a crust or deposit which makes decanting necessary; such old *Crusted Ports* are highly prized. While maturing in the bottle, a certain flaky substance called "beeswing" is often formed, but this affects the taste of the wine not at all and is looked on as a good omen, indicating a rich, old wine. Port is sometimes made from white grapes, to produce *White Port* that is extremely pale in color, but the deeper tones of the red ports are much preferred in England, where Port is best known.

Port is a magnificent drink with which to end a meal, and excellent with many desserts or as a substitute for them. But Port is most customarily served after a meal is ended, with nuts and cheese, the bottle traditionally being passed clockwise around the table. Port has a particular affinity to melons, and there is perhaps no better summer dessert than a juicy moon of melon and a glass of well-matured Port.

Port vintages shipped in the past few years have included 1945, 1947, and 1948, which produced excellent wines, followed by 1950, 1954, 1955, and 1958. Earlier vintages include 1942 and 1934 and 1935, still being drunk. In the past decade, vintages have been 1960 and 1963, the last not being ready until the nineties.

LEADING PORT SHIPPERS

Burmester	Feuerheerd
Butler, Nephew	Fonseca
Cockburn, Smithes	Graham
Croft	Kopke
Da Silva	Mackenzie
Delaforce	Sandeman
Dow	Smith Woodhouse
Ferreira	Taylor, Fladgate
	Warre

MADEIRA

The island of Madeira, off the African bulge and out in the Atlantic, is also a Portuguese possession, and during Revolutionary days no wine was more famous. Madeiras range from the dry *Sercials* through the light and slightly sweet *Bual*, to the rich, dark *Malmsey*, sometimes called *Malvasia*, and the dark *Verdelho*, which is made from white grapes. The wines are named after the grape varieties from which they are made. All have a tonic taste of iron and continue to develop in cask, becoming more intense with the passing of each decade. Like the Port wine trade, the Madeira trade is in the hands of the English, although the Scandinavian countries account for most of today's consumption.

The wines are stored in glasshouses, hot rooms called *estufadas*, that are held at high temperatures for weeks and then are allowed to cool, darkening the wine. This baking is the way imitation Sherries are made in wine regions outside Europe, so that a so-called "Sherry" from American, Australian, or South African producers should more properly be called Madeira.

Madeiras are generally served between meals or with desserts, although the dry Sercials make excellent drinks before dinner.

LEADING MADEIRA SHIPPERS

Blandy's	Kopke
Cossart, Gordon	Leacock
Henriques & Henriques	Shortridge, Lawton

186

OTHER FORTIFIED WINES

Other fortified wines, whose fermentation is stopped by a dosage of brandy to preserve some of the natural grape sugar, include the Malaga of southern Spain, deep and red and luscious, the Marsala of Sicily, which is sweet and darkly rich, and the Muscatels. Muscat grapes are grown in every warm wine-growing country, producing rich wines that are often sweetened and fortified, but these rarely have the distinction of a Port, Sherry, or Madeira. In Spain, a sweet wine is made from the Pedro Ximenez grape, where it is called P.X.; this wine is used to sweeten and darken the Oloroso, but quantities of it are often aged in a *solera* system, and produce a dark, rich wine similar to Malaga. They are rarely exported. With Sherry, Port, and Madeira so readily available, there is small demand for other types of fortified wines. The exceptions are the imitation Sherries and Ports, the cheapest forms of alcohol on the market, generally, and these are extremely popular, even though they have little or no similarity to the great wines of Spain and Portugal.

Appendix

BUYING WINES IN RESTAURANTS. Restaurants charge two and three times the retail price of a bottle of wine, and it's a reckless man or a foolish one who doesn't resent paying six dollars for a wine that should cost two, or eighteen for a bottle of Champagne that normally costs six. Many places don't like to serve wines because sipping makes people dawdle, and that slows up table turnover.

What restaurants ought to do, of course, is to take a retailer's markup, plus a charge for serving the wine. Such a corkage would be relatively the same for an expensive wine as for a cheap one, which would make it possible to buy top wines in restaurants, not inexpensive ones.

Prices being what they are, good wines that are available in large quantity and therefore inexpensive are the most sensible ones to buy when dining out. Among reds, a Côtes du Rhône or a Beaujolais is generally a good choice, if you want a French wine, stepping up to a Côte de Beaune or a minor Bordeaux Château if a wine of more age and delicacy is wanted. Zinfandel or one of the other varietals from California or New York is often a good buy. As for whites, a Muscadet from the Loire or a Pouilly-Fuissé from southern Burgundy is usually a good buy. If Swiss wines were more widely distributed, they would probably be the best dry white buys. Alsatian or German regionals are good buys when you want a flowery wine, although some of the Italian whites can be reasonable in price, as can the reds. Italian reds, though, are generally low in quality when they are low in price.

Wine stewards, called *sommeliers* in the top French restaurants, sometimes know about wines and sometimes don't, but at least they will be familiar with the wines in the restaurant cellar, and which of them are apt to go best with the specialties of the house. Sometimes, too, they can point out wines that are features of the restaurant, and often not marked up as high as others on the list.

Wine cards are often fancy on the outside and skimpy on the inside. A good way to judge them is to note how many estate-bottled Burgundies and Classed Growths of Bordeaux are on the list. If there are half a dozen of each in several good vintages that are old enough to drink, then you can probably trust most of the other wines listed. There should be a good representative selection from the French and German regions, and some wines from Italy, Switzerland and Spain, California and New York.

The waiter or wine steward should pour some wine in the glass of the person who selected the bottle, who should then smell the wine to see that it is good. If there's anything unpleasant—the slightest trace of corky smell, or a lot of sulphur—the wine should be rejected. If there's some doubt, the wine ought to be tasted, and if there's anything unpleasant in the taste, back goes the wine to the steward. A good steward won't give any argument; if he does, ask him to call the captain; if the captain offers any sort of argument, finish your meal as calmly as you can, in case you don't want to walk out. In any case, cross the restaurant off your list, because it doesn't know its business, and there are plenty of fine restaurants across the country that do.

CORKY BOTTLES. Corks occasionally dry up, and the wine takes on the smell and taste of cork. Such wines are undrinkable, and will always be accepted as a return by a reputable merchant or wine steward. Corkiness is easy to detect; all one has to do is to smell the cork. If the cork smells of wine, the wine is not corky. If there's the slightest whiff of cork, the wine is bad.

MADERIZATION. Old white wines have a tendency to oxidize, or rust, taking on a musty taste of straw something like the taste of Madeira. It appears in white wines that may be only two or three years old, especially when the wine has been badly kept or when it is one of the soft wines of the south. Usually, of course, dry white wines live for five years or longer, and sweet white wines often last much longer. A maderized wine begins to turn the color of straw, then change to brown, losing all its character. Nothing tastes worse. Send it back.

SULPHUR IN WINES. All wines are protected by sulphur, which is used in the vineyards and in wine making to fight various illnesses that can attack a wine. White wines, particularly, are sometimes too heavily sulphured, so that the wine tastes of sulphur. One taste of sulphur and one can't taste wine for hours. A whiff of sulphur will sometimes disappear after the wine has been opened awhile, but usually if the sulphur can be smelled, the wine will be unpleasant to drink.

STORING WINES. Wines suffer from temperature change and vibration, so a cool (55°–65°), quiet place is the best place to store wines. The storage can be warmer if the wines are going to be drunk up in a matter of months, even up to 70° as long as it does not fluctuate. Wines are usually laid on their sides, so that the cork will keep wet and not shrink. Aside from these precautions, no special care is needed. Within their limits, wines are remarkably sturdy.

VINTAGE CHARTS. Except for the greatest wines, vintages are not particularly important. Charts are useless for even the great wines because the weather varies so much, and because a man who picks late will make a different wine from the man who picks too soon. One vineyard may have old vines, another may have young ones, and the wine will be quite different. Vintage charts must be too general to give any more than the most superficial indications as to quality. They are best ignored unless they go into some detail, district by district.

GLASSES. A wineglass ought to be half chimney, so that the smell of the wine is collected in the top of the glass, and should be clear, so that the wine can be admired. The best wineglasses are shaped like a tulip, and at least six or eight ounces in capacity, even larger ones being pleasant to drink from. A stem isn't necessary—stemware is pleasing to hold, and wine looks good in it. The average serving of wine, no matter how large the glass, is three or four ounces.

ORDER OF SERVING WINES. Dry wines taste best before sweet ones, young before old, white before red, light before full.

WHISTLING IN. The smell and taste of wine are contained in what are called the volatiles, those properties that are released when the alcohol in a wine evaporates. For that reason swirling the glass brings out the smell of the wine, and the same matter of getting air at the alcohol to cause it to evaporate helps when one tastes a wine. An expert takes about half a teaspoonful of wine in his mouth, then sucks in air to cause the alcohol to evaporate, releasing the qualities of the wine, and to bounce the wine around in the mouth so that it is brought into touch with all the taste buds. The process is called whistling in, and makes a cheerfully vulgar sound that is not only considered proper, but also a sort of perpetual protest against wine snobbery.

CORKSCREWS. The best corkscrews are spirals of wire, rather than a spiral that has cutting edges which can chew up a cork. The point should be in a line with the coil, not in the center, so that the wire can follow the point into the cork. The corkscrew, not the bottle, is twisted when the cork is pulled, so that the wine won't be unnecessarily joggled.

DECANTING. Wines rarely need decanting these days, being carefully filtered before bottling. Sediment doesn't hurt a wine at all, and the trick is to pour the wine off the sediment before it is to be served. This is a simple matter of pouring the wine slowly into another container at eye level, so that you can see when the sediment begins to follow the wine from the bottle.

BASKETS. There are all sorts of cradles for bottles, and most of them are pretentious. A bottle is a perfect device for pouring, and gadgets only complicate the simple process. The only possible excuse for a basket would be the need for pouring gently an old wine full of sediment.

BOTTLE SIZES. The bigger the bottle, the more slowly the wine matures. Half bottles of a wine that would normally take five years to mature may be ready to drink in three or four. On the other hand wines in magnums, double bottles, develop more slowly and more completely. Magnums are the perfect size for dinner parties and large gatherings, and half bottles are the wines for those times when a glass or two would taste wonderful and any more would be too much.

WINE TEMPERATURES. White and pink wines taste best cool, somewhere around 50°, but lose much of their flavor when they are a great deal colder than that. An hour on the bottom shelf of a refrigerator is about the length of time needed for cooling. Sudden chilling in the ice compartment may tend to make the wine taste flabby. The fruity, young red wines of the south usually taste

best at cellar temperature, perhaps about 60°. Old wines
and great ones taste best at what used to be considered
room temperature, say, 65° to 75°, but even old red
wines taste insipid when they are much warmer than
that.

Index

INDEX

199

202

206

216

M

EUROPEAN WINE REGIONS AND DISTRICTS

FRANCE

BORDEAUX
1. Médoc
2. Pomerol
3. St. Émilion
4. Graves
5. Sauternes

BURGUNDY
1. Chablis
2. Côte de Nuits
   Fixin
   Gevrey
   Morey
   Chambolle
   Vougeot
   Flagey
   Vosne
   Nuits
3. Côte de Beaune
   Aloxe
   Savigny
   Beaune
   Pommard
   Volnay
   Monthelie
   Meursault
   Puligny
   Chassagne
   Santenay
4. Chalonnais
5. Maconnais
6. Beaujolais

RHÔNE
1. Côte Rôtie
2. Hermitage
3. Châteauneuf-du-Pape
4. Tavel

LOIRE
1. Muscadet
2. Anjou
3. Saumur
4. Bourgueil
5. Chinon
6. Vouvray
7. Reuilly & Quincy
8. Sancerre &
   Pouilly-sur-Loire

LOIRE

BAY OF BISCAY

BORDEAUX

FRANCE

RIOJA

PORTUGAL

PÔRTO

SPAIN

SHERRY
Manzanilla
Fino
Amontillado
Oloroso

JEREZ

MALAGA

ALGERIA